THE DANKTIONARY

AN A–Z GUIDE TO STONER SLANG

WILL B. HIGH

adamsmedia

AVON, MASSACHUSETTS

Published by Adams Media, a division of F+W Media, Inc. 57 Littlefield Street, Avon, MA 02322. U.S.A. www.adamsmedia.com

This book is an abridgement of Weedopedia: A Totally Dank A–Z Reefer Reference by Will B. High, copyright © 2010 by F+W Media, Inc., ISBN 10: 1-4405-0645-0, ISBN 13: 978-1-4405-0645-1.

ISBN 10: 1-4405-2812-8
ISBN 13: 978-1-4405-2812-5

Printed in the United States of America.

10   9   8   7   6   5   4   3   2   1

Library of Congress Cataloging-in-Publication Data
is available from the publisher.

Introduction

Marijuana—biological genus category cannabis sativa, cannabis indica, and cannabis ruderalis—is a medically relevant, recreationally useful, naturally grown narcotic of the safest and most benign kind.

The average pot smoker is also pretty benign and wants nothing more than to be able to unwind with a joint at the end of the day (or even at the beginning) without being lectured by the hall monitors of society.

Which is the risk you run if you ask someone, "Dude, what's a 420?" And that is why this definitive guide to stoner slang exists.

Compiled here are many entries (we didn't have the intensity of focus to count them all) that cover the entire spectrum of stoner slang. There's also an appendix that gives the low-down on munchies, since all true stoners feel the need to nosh. Like stoners themselves, this encyclopedia is lighthearted, nonthreatening, self-deprecating, and genuinely fun to have around.

As with most endeavors, this tome is best enjoyed with an open mind, a burning joint, and a strong desire to learn everything one could possibly want to know about the lexicon of marijuana. We hope to enlighten, entertain, share some laughs, and make some memories together. Most of all, we just hope to stay on topic.

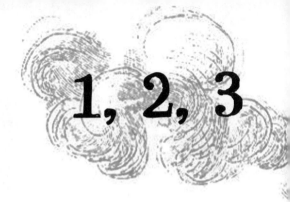

1, 2, 3

4 Way, a sexual ménage à trois (plus one), or a strand of marijuana that is a crossbreed of four potent strains. 4 Way is frequently advertised on marijuana seed-selling websites as a supergroup of marijuana product, taking only the best from four different strands and putting them all together in a new strand. Not surprisingly, 4 Way weed is typically about as enjoyable as a supergroup—good, but not as good as the originals, kind of like Blind Faith. Nevertheless, it still is a great strand to have in case the opportunity ever comes up to drop the line, "So, want to have a 4 Way . . . let me finish . . . blunt."

42, the answer to life, the universe, and everything, as defined in *The Hitchhiker's Guide to the Galaxy*. While the answer is known, unfortunately the question remains a mystery, especially to stoners. Their possible theories include: "How many roads must a man walk down?" "How many stoners does it take to screw in a lightbulb?" "What is 420 divided by ten?" "How many hits are too many?"

© 2011 www.clipart.com

420, a term used to declare oneself a part of the pot-smoking culture by saying one is "420 friendly" or, more bluntly, "Let's smoke some 420." It is perhaps one of the most misunderstood marijuana terms, as several urban legends exist to explain its origin. Some claim it derives from the penal code section in California for marijuana use. It doesn't. Others claim it is the number of chemical compounds in marijuana. It's not. Some mistakenly believe it's the date Jim Morrison died or the room The Grateful Dead always stayed in on tour. Nope. In fact the term derives from a group of pothead high-schoolers at San Rafael High School in California who used it as a reminder for the time they planned to toke up. Really. Yeah, kind of disappointing.

See also 420 celebrations; light up; pack a bowl; spark

420 Celebrations, an annual pothead holiday falling on April 20 meant to celebrate the rich culture of marijuana smoking. In actuality it's just another excuse to get high. Usually the day involves college-campus potheads emptying onto the streets to blast music, smoke weed, wear their newly washed tie-dyed shirts, and wish each other a "Happy 420." Some events have political overtones in supporting decriminalization efforts, but the rest of the world never takes it seriously. Vancouver hosts one of the most heavily attended events, and it's not uncommon to see friendly smokers throwing free joints to the crowd; the hippie version of throwing out free T-shirts at a basketball game.

See also 420

50-Yard Line, a long white strip of powder that separates one half of a football field from the other. In one of the final scenes of the stoner film *Dazed and Confused*, several of the main characters share a joint on this portion of the field, which has resulted in millions of stoners replicating this experience at high schools around the world. In theory it is a terrible place to

© istockphoto / jlsohio

smoke: It's out in the open, there's usually only one exit, and it's near a school so the penalty if one is caught is often more severe. However, there is a certain sense of satisfaction to giving a metaphorical middle finger to one's local high school and sparking up a fatty right in plain sight.

99 Cent Store, the greatest store ever to someone high. If it is a true ninety-nine cent store, everything is only ninety-nine cents. Invisible ink, plastic handcuffs, sassy bumper stickers, toy soldiers, fake mustaches, goggly-eye glasses, paper plates, sudoku books, whoopee cushions, tennis balls, and every off-brand candy and snack one could dream of. Stoners can spend an entire evening walking up and down the aisles, leave with bags full of munchies and novelty items, and still have enough money to buy an eighth. And they often do just that.

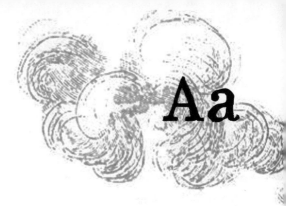

Aa

Active Stoner, a contradiction of sorts, this variety of stoner likes nothing more than to get high and seize the day. For most smokers, post-toking activities like hiking, bike riding, marathon running, and cross-country skiing sound like buzzkills, but the active stoner actually seeks out these sorts of physical activities as a means to enhance the high. It is best that active stoners keep to their own kind, as their trademark enthusiasm and get-up-and-go attitude are sure to bother anyone who was under the impression that the day would be spent sitting around watching Cartoon Network.

See also enhancement stoner; handy stoner; intellectual stoner; lazy stoner; social stoner; stoner; talkative stoner

Adult Swim, an eight-or-so-hour block of mindless, shamelessly lowbrow TV that weedheads can proudly call their own. Airing in the postmidnight to presunup hours on Cartoon Network, *Adult Swim* is the epitome of stupid humor (in the best way) designed and explicitly intended for consumption by the stoned and spaced out. The programming block contains such stoner favorites as *Aqua Teen Hunger Force*; *Tim and Eric Awesome Show, Great Job!*; and *Robot Chicken.* Uncontrollable fits of laughter for reasons even the viewer is unaware of are common. Contemplating what makes the shows funny is equally frequent and extremely puzzling. Luckily the majority of the programs last only a few minutes, so if one does not understand what's going on, it will be over soon enough.

Afghan Kush, a desirable strain of marijuana indigenous to areas of Afghanistan, Turkmenistan, Uzbekistan, and Tajikistan, all actual countries. The first strains hit the U.S. market in the mid-1970s and have remained strongly favored since. Authentic Afghan Kush can run about $600 an ounce and is not intended for novices. The high can be described as heavy and hard-hitting and can pound smokers into a two-hour, couch-sitting, blank-eyed submission of the best kind.

See also **kush**

Ali G, the ganja-loving, grammatically challenged brainchild of comedian Sasha Baron Cohen and host of the now-defunct HBO series *Da Ali G Show*. Perhaps Ali G's most classic pot-related moment came while interviewing a U.S. Drug Enforcement Agency officer. Ali G: "What is the different types of hash out there? We all know that it's called the bionic, the bomb, the puff, the blow, the black, the herb, the sensi, the chronic, the sweet Mary Jane, the shit, ganja, split, reefer, the bad, the Buddha, the homegrown, the ill, the Maui-Maui, the method, pot, lethal, turbo, tie, shake, skunk, stress, wacky, weed, glaze, the boot, dime bag, Scooby Doo, bob, bogey, backyard boogie. But what is the other terms for it?" DEA guy: "That just about covers it."

Amusement Parks, locations of fun consisting of roller coasters, kiddie rides, waterslides, overpriced food, awkward photo shoots, and long lines. They are oftentimes isolated from centers of commerce because of their large scale and the completely unique universe they occupy. Amusement parks are known to have their own currency and give unfettered authority to sixteen-year-old kids. They are also not responsible for lost or stolen things. Amusement parks are common places for stoners to hang out, and as such they have crack security on-site at all times, busting meddlesome and largely unthreatening teenagers. If security knew what was best, they'd let the teenagers go free, spend $40

for two pizzas and a coke, and then hurl upon the completion—or perhaps in the middle—of the new X-Men ride.

Antisocial Stoner, a breed of pot enthusiast who prefers to smoke in seclusion. They are prone to bouts of introspection and contemplation and are significantly less likely to come up with highdeas, which are generally a symptom of groupthink. It's not that they are elitists. They just prefer to get high and ponder the great mysteries of the universe without being interrupted by a group of cackling idiots who just realized *God* is *dog* spelled backward. On second thought, perhaps they are elitists.

See also artistic stoner; closet stoner; hungry stoner; intellectual stoner; lazy stoner; paranoid stoner; quiet stoner; social stoner; stoner

Apple Pipe, a makeshift but perfectly serviceable novelty contraption. The pipe is used primarily for smoking in public places because of the harmless look of a piece of fruit in someone's hand, as well as the ease with which it can be disposed of, if necessary. Apple pipes mimic the chamber system of

© istockphoto / DNY59

a typical pipe: one long chamber across the width of the apple and a half-drilled chamber to place a finger on while inhaling. The apple pipe is surprisingly effective, easy to make, and gives its user a sense of joy and accomplishment upon completion. Another benefit: It can be eaten when those munchies suddenly kick in.

See also foil pipe; highlighter pipe; hot knifing

Artistic Stoner, a variety of pot smoker who will often use the drug as a means of boosting his or her creativity. At first, the incorporation of marijuana is simply an enhancement to the creative process. Before long, however, artistic stoners can become incapable of producing any meaningful painting, sculpture, song, or sonnet without the benefit of marijuana. Often they are also incapable of producing anything meaningful even with the help of cannabis. However, this usually goes unnoticed by them.

See also antisocial stoner; enhancement stoner; intellectual stoner; quiet stoner; social stoner; stoner

Bb

Babysitting, a slang term used to describe the act of holding on to a joint, bowl, bong, or other marijuana delivery mechanism for an inordinate amount of time without the intention of actually smoking it. Unlike some instances of marijuana hoarding like bogarting and leeching, babysitting is generally unintentional and entered into without malice. The subject is often caught up in recounting an important story, stuffing his or her face with munchies, or is unable to remember the third portion of the "puff, puff, pass" method of smoking. Similar to a traditional babysitter, the subject will often seem catatonic and take little interest in what's going on around him or her. This is normal and can be easily remedied with a sharp object, loud music, or two fingers rubbed together in a snapping motion.

Baggie, a plastic sandwich bag of varying size in which weed is frequently distributed. Baggies are usually sold as eighths but smaller bags are used to hold seeds as well. The baggie is practical on all fronts. It's a reliable way to ensure no marijuana is lost during transfer, it's freezer safe for storing purposes, and it's easy to open, allowing each buyer the time-honored tradition of buying the bag, unsealing the flap, taking a quick whiff and emitting a satisfying, "Ahhhhhhhh, that smells good."

See also dealers; dime bag; eighth; nickel bag

Baked, a slang term used to describe somebody who has consumed marijuana in some way, shape, or form and is now high. Really high. Symptoms include bloodshot eyes, inexplicable and insatiable hunger, decreased attention span when performing important tasks, increased attention span when performing unimportant tasks, short-term memory loss, heightened ability to contemplate life's great mysteries, and a general feeling of euphoria.

See also high; ripped; stoned; wasted; zonked

Bananadine, a fictional drug which many people once believed could be extracted from banana peels. Originally intended as a satirical jab at the American government's overactive legislation of psychoactive chemicals, the Bananadine myth first appeared in the form of an extraction recipe featured in the *Berkeley Barb*, a politically active underground newspaper. Though many readers got the joke, William Powell, author of *The Anarchist Cookbook*, did not. He published the fallacious recipe in the cookbook, which led to a profusion of rumors that Donovan's hit song "Mellow Yellow," released before the *Barb's* article was even published, was all about the singer's penchant for the smooth, fruity high. The resulting cultural collision resulted in a ridiculous fad in which gullible stoners rode out wicked placebo effects while smoking banana peels.

See also **K2**

Basements, subterranean extensions of modern homes used to store boxes of crap, bicycles, power tools, and degenerate twenty-somethings who can't seem to get a job despite possessing a philosophy degree from a rather expensive university. When not rifling through the boxes of crap, the degenerate twenty-somethings will often use the space as a secluded place to smoke pot with other degenerate twenty-somethings.

While there are numerous products one can purchase to deal with pest problems like cockroaches or mice, there is currently no spray or trap on the market to help a homeowner deal with a stoner infestation.

Beach, The, a sandy location near a large body of water where individuals go to smoke, relax, suntan, swim, play volleyball, surf, dig holes, and look at the scantily clad beach patrons. Surfers, especially, are known to smoke the ganja, as their wild, long hair and laid-back attitudes are just the sort of things stoners are known for. But for commoners, the beach can still be a place to enjoy a blunt. Some activities to enjoy while at the beach and high: floating in the water as the waves pass by, getting buried in sand, skipping stones, drinking Coronas, buying Freeze-E-Pops, letting sand pour through one's fingers, playing a ukulele, collecting seashells, and of course trying to stop oneself from staring directly into the sun.

Bionic, an adjective in broad English usage that describes something related to the field of bionics. More specifically, an artificial process that reproduces and enhances normal biological processes, such as a mechanical arm or RoboCop. As such, it has been adapted by the pot-smoking community as a noun to refer to bud, as it enhances the normal biological process of sitting around and doing nothing.

© istockphoto / scibak

Blunt, a popular method for smoking pot in large groups. A blunt is rolled using special rolling papers or the more popular method of "gutting" an inexpensive cigar, discarding the tobacco, and rerolling it with marijuana. There is some debate over which direction the blunt moves from person to person, but the "puff, puff, pass" rule is a widely accepted term of etiquette. It is interesting to note that this rule is almost always forgotten by at least one smoker in any given group. Because the remainder of the circle is generally too high to notice, this is rarely an issue.

See also **blunt cruising; Dutch Master; shotgun**

Blunt cruising, the act of driving a car while smoking joints with friends. Always seems like a way better idea beforehand than when the high-speed police chase starts. And especially when it ends. Blunt cruising usually results in two or three friends blasting music, passing a joint or blunt, and screaming their faces off with one friend driving, hunched over and completely focused on never going even one mile per hour over the speed limit. Despite the driver's laserlike focus, blunt cruising is the No. 1 cause of lost side mirrors. Always best to blunt cruise when traffic is low. Also, it is wise to stick to those highways with divots that make a noise when the car starts drifting off the road, as that'll tend to happen.

See also **blunt**

Blurrito, a blunt made from a burrito shell.

Bogart (for the famous 1940s actor, see another encyclopedia), a rather negative slang term directed at someone who missed the key developmental stage of childhood in which humans learn to share. Somebody who Bogarts might take too long with his or her turn on a joint, or might even go so far as to horde a cache of marijuana in secret and claim to be fresh out when it comes time to contribute. In general, pot smokers are passive and congenial. However, an instance of bogarting will inevitably elicit the most vile insult a stoner is capable of delivering: "Yo dude, not cool."

See also **buzzkiller; leech**

Bomb, a term used to describe a grade of pot so high that it will blow a smoker's mind. Not specific to a certain strain or kind, bomb can be used to describe any high-grade weed. Avoid using while watching news coverage of war, as smokers may bug out from realizing its multilayered application.

Bong, a decadent piece of paraphernalia used for smoking marijuana that often contains ornate designs and colors. Often, smokers will impart human names and characteristics to their bongs and treat them far better than they do most actual humans. This behavior is considered to be normal and is generally encouraged within the pot-smoking community.

See *also* gravity bong; party bong; piece

Bong Water, a substance found in most bongs, consisting of ordinary H20 mixed with trace amounts of ash, marijuana, THC particles, and an element indefinable by modern science called "gross." Bong water acts as a cooling agent that reduces the temperature of marijuana smoke before it reaches the lungs, thus making it possible to hold large quantities of smoke in the lungs for a longer period of time. While it does perform this useful purpose, it is generally understood to be a vile by-product of the smoking experience that will stain anything it comes into contact with. Under no circumstances should one attempt to imbibe bong water unless one is being forced to do so at gunpoint or unless one has lost a bet.

See *also* water

Bowl, a relatively small item made of glass, plastic, wood, or ceramic, used to smoke marijuana. However, if parents, police officers, or other persons of authority ask, it's actually an intricate sculpture with no practical use whatsoever. In many states, bowls are perfectly legal to own and sell as long as they are purchased for use solely with tobacco products. The feigned ignorance punctuated by exaggerated winking necessary to purchase a bowl is pretty humiliating but still infinitely better than smoking out of a soda can.

See also piece

© istockphoto / SleepyMonkey

Boxing, or to Box Out, the act of hotboxing an enclosed space. For example: "Hey, let's box the shit out of my brother's motorcycle helmet!"

See also hotbox

Brick, a large compact bar of marijuana that typically weighs either one pound or one kilogram, depending on the country of origin. Pot is bundled in this manner for ease of shipment and subsequent storage, as it is much easier to stack a box full of bricks than it is a box full of glass jars. If one should ever happen to come across a brick, it is best to push all thoughts of running off with it out of one's head. Just leave it alone. While it would certainly be enough pot to last a couple of months, those would likely be the last months of one's life. The owner of said brick might just use a real, far more painful brick as a means for getting it back.

Brown, Bobby, former member of the group New Edition, solo pop star, and legally troubled ex-husband of singer Whitney Houston. Brown's ignoble history has turned him into one of the late-night circuit's most reliable punch lines and one of the pot-smoking circuit's most insulting descriptors. Any low-grade, dried-up, headache-inducing schwag can be distinguished as Bobby Brown. If a smoker claims, "This is some Bobby Brown shit" during a smokeout, immediately apologize and buy some new stuff ASAP.

Bubbleberry, a strain of marijuana derived by combining characteristics from bubblegum and blueberry varieties. For the average smoker, pot is pot. For marijuana connoisseurs, the flavors and varieties available in strains like Bubbleberry are as abundant and unique as in fine wines. Similar to wine snobs, it is not uncommon for pot aficionados to develop preferences based on subtle flavor differences undetectable to those who don't possess a particularly sophisticated palate. Among these sommeliers of the pot world, Bubbleberry is highly regarded as both potent and pleasant to smoke. It is also generally more expensive than other varieties of marijuana, so great care should be taken as to when and how it is smoked. There's no sense in cracking open a pricey single-malt scotch for shot number twenty on a friend's twenty-first birthday. The same rules apply to weed.

See also **Northern Lights; Purple Haze; White Widow**

Bubbler, a glass smoking device with a pouch under the chamber where cold water can be placed to cool the smoke as it is inhaled. Bubblers fall somewhere between a pipe and a bong on the smoking-device evolutionary chain. While the bubbler adds the cooling effect that a pipe lacks, it fails to incorporate the slide of a bong. Still, some smokers prefer bubblers because they're smaller, easier to transport, lighter-weight and easier to hide from the fuzz.

See also **bong; piece**

Bud, one of the thousands of slang terms for marijuana and among the most common. Bud works on two tracks. Bud is short for a buddy, which marijuana certainly is. Bud is also a botanical term for an undeveloped flower, which marijuana technically is not, but since it's a plant it still kind of works.

© istockphoto / Mac99

See also **Buddha; ganja; Mary Jane; pot; reefer**

Buddha, an enlightened being in the Buddhist religion often depicted as a serene, portly gentleman sitting cross-legged. In some cultures, it is also a euphemism for marijuana. The link between the green leafy substance and achieving ultimate spiritual oneness makes absolute sense to anyone who has ever gotten high and little to no sense to anyone who hasn't.

See also bud; ganja; Mary Jane; pot; reefer

Bummer, a slang term used by stoners and surfers to express disappointment in the outcome of a given situation. The term is especially versatile, as it can be used after any range of unfortunate incidents from minor inconveniences like running out of weed to major life events like the death of a close family member. This does not necessarily mean the average stoner sees running out of pot as being on par with losing a loved one; however, it's certainly pretty bad. It's at least as bad as losing a pet hamster that one didn't particularly care for in the first place.

Burnt Out, a state of being after a particularly intense session of smoking pot which can become permanent if one continues to smoke with the same level of reckless abandon. Symptoms include droopy bloodshot eyes, cotton mouth, oversleeping, general contentment with life, and an intense desire to continue getting high.

© istockphoto / vasiliki

See also **perma-burned**

Buzzed, the initial state of being high achieved after a minimal ingestion of smoke from the cannabis sativa plant. Many argue that this state of being is the most pleasant type of high, as one is still relatively coherent and has not yet achieved a status of baked or stoned.

See also **baked; high; stoned**

Buzzkiller, any number of people, places, objects, or events that can completely and utterly ruin the experience of getting high. They should be avoided at all costs while high and can include, but are not limited to: police officers or anyone of any level of authority, parental units, large crowds (excluding concerts, orgies, and protests), bogarting, ex-boyfriends/girlfriends, unexpected encounters with coworkers, running out of pot, running out of munchies, younger siblings, midterms, and diet pop.

See also bogart; narc; volcano

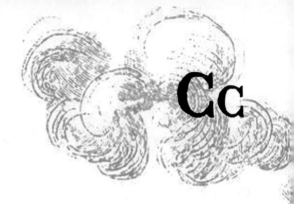

Cc

Can Bong, the minimalist's makeshift bong, since it can be made simply with an empty beer or soda can and a sharp object. One creates a can bong by denting an empty can, poking small holes through the dent (where the pot will sit), and poking a hole in the bottom of the can to use as a carb. The user then inhales smoke through the can opening. Not the most highbrow smoking contraption, can bongs are still a rite of passage for the high school smoker and an easy way to prove one's credibility as a resourceful weedhead. The practice of can bong-making becomes increasingly pathetic with age.

See also **apple pipe; foil pipe; highlighter pipe**

Canoeing (to Canoe), when a novice is sparking a joint and burns one side more than the other. The resultant heat differential produces a canoe-shaped jay, which is not cool. The appropriate course of action is to shout "Bro! It's canoeing!" and apply flame to the opposite side, bringing the joint, and the session, back to equilibrium.

See also **joint**

Cannabis, the wacky tabacky, sticky icky, devil's lettuce, Mary Jane, green rooster, bud, envy, trees, or any other of the unlimited names that describe the magical plant. In fact, smokers tend to call it *anything* but "cannabis," and it is mostly DEA officers, poorly trained narcs, judges, scientists, and botanists who employ the term. Smokers who use the term are usually engaging in a discussion with one of those officials regarding the drug's legal status or its effects on human health. It's known to cause red eyes, dry mouth, an increased heart rate, and extremely desirable intoxication.

See also **every entry in this encyclopedia**

Cannonball, a self-induced challenge performed by stoners wherein one inhales a large quantity of marijuana smoke, takes a full shot of hard liquor, and then exhales the hit. When done properly, the stunt is harmless, albeit a little immature. When timed poorly,

© 2011 www.clipart.com

however, this can result in aspirated liquor being sprayed all over everyone else in the room. It is customary to finish the maneuver by shouting "Cannonball!" at the top of one's lungs before passing both pot and liquor to the next willing participant. While this step is not required, the whole process is just kind of silly without it.

See also **strikeout**

Carb, a hole in a bubbler or a pipe that allows the user to clear the smoke in the chamber by increasing the volume of air that flows into the device. First proposed by Dutch-Swiss mathematician/confirmed pothead Daniel Bernoulli, whose pioneering work in fluid mechanics was widely read by stoners in his 1738 book *Hydrodynamica*. Further evidence that drug technology proceeds at a far faster pace than the clean world: Karl Benz didn't patent the automotive carburetor until 1886.

See also **bubbler; pipe**

Carmelicious, a strain of weed that is green with orange hairs sticking out of it and can give a distinctly caramel taste when smoked or smelled. Carmelicious is a favorite among beginner growers, as it's relatively easy to grow and it produces a happy high. The buds are sticky and heavy. Best of all, grandmothers always have a bowl of Carmelicious available on their coffee tables, though, beware—sometimes they're mixed with old jelly beans and stale chocolate.

Casual Stoner, a person who will participate in an occasional smoking session but does not feel the need to indulge in the practice on a regular basis. He or she is unlikely to possess a personal stash of marijuana, although the casual stoner will gladly contribute munchies or money toward the cause—a defining characteristic that separates such stoners from leeches.

See also antisocial stoner; closet stoner; quiet stoner; social stoner; stoner; talkative stoner

Cellar Door, a phrase popularized in *Donnie Darko*, a 2001 dark comedy starring Jake and Maggie Gyllenhaal, Drew Barrymore, and a giant invisible bunny. The movie involves love, time travel, alternate realities, several real and unreal deaths, and a school flooding. It's trippy, scary, and, upon first viewing, completely nonsensical, making it an instant stoner classic. The Drew Barrymore character explains that the phrase "cellar door" is an example of what some people consider the most beautiful-sounding phrase in the English language. High school stoners are likely to make "cellar door" a Facebook status or message board user name. When asked what their favorite movies are, 100 percent of high school stoners will place *Donnie Darko* toward the top of the list. That number drops to 25 percent of college stoners, and hovers just around whatever the unemployment rate happens to be postcollege.

Cereal box, a common hiding spot for weed. It's inconspicuous, totally ordinary looking, and gives breakfasts that extra aroma that Count Chocula was always missing. Cereal boxes occasionally end up in odd places when they're storing weed. As a result, unsuspecting clients will arrive at their drug dealer's house, open the freezer, and ask why there's a cereal box waiting inside. When faced with this odd circumstance, it is usually best just to pretend as if one sees cereal boxes in the freezer all the time.

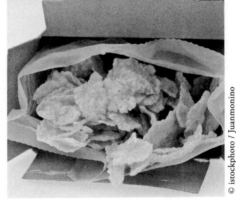

© istockphoto / Juanmonino

Chamber, the hollow area of any pot-smoking apparatus that is used to collect smoke before it is inhaled into the lungs, where it belongs. The larger the chamber, the more smoke can accumulate, and the more high the user will get from each hit. However, it is often speculated that individuals who purchase absurdly large bongs and pipes are merely compensating for other areas in which they are lacking.

See also bong

Champagne, a strain of weed popularly grown in outdoor gardens due to its relatively mild stench. Champagne is also popular due to its strength, which will cause some stoners to declare it the "best pot I've ever smoked!" though this claim is often made by the sort of people who declare the most recent book they've read is their favorite book of all time. Champagne shouldn't be discounted, though. One fat joint can make five or six smokers very happy, as the weed gives a clear-headed sort of high. The strain is also a favorite of baseball players, who shake it up and pour it all over each other and smoke the hell out of it while giving postgame interviews upon clinching a playoff berth.

Cheeseburgers, pseudonym for quarter ounce of marijuana. Better than McDonald's. Not as good as White Castle.

Cherry, the smoldering ember of delicious THC-laden marijuana that rests at the end of a joint or blunt. Once the end of the joint or blunt is lit, the cherry will continue to ignite the marijuana resting behind it, which will then become the cherry. This process continues until the joint is finished or until some asshole interrupts it by ashing too hard and knocking the cherry on the ground.

See also **blunt; joint**

Chillum, a one-hitter of Indian origin used by wandering Hindu monks in their quest to unlock all the backward racetracks in *Mario Kart 64*. Their dogmatic devotion to the 64-bit processor led to their eventual decline.

See also **one-hitter; pipe**

Christmas Tree, a variety of marijuana whose pinelike smell, fuzzy texture, and white-sprinkly, snowflakelike exterior makes it a natural choice for the holiday shopper. Christmas Tree is seasonal, grown in sunny California, and is among the most potent strands of marijuana in the United States. It has been a source of some controversy lately, as local governments are trying to get the phrase "Holiday tree" to catch on to be more inclusive. Still, Christmas Tree is a rare and strong breed, up to three times as expensive as regular bud. It makes for the perfect stocking stuffer.

See also **Bubbleberry; Northern Lights; Purple Haze**

Chrondola, a stoner's nickname for the gondola at a ski mountain. A cozy enclosed space with privacy for a single toker and five of his or her snowboarding buddies. Similar to the chairlift, the apparatus moves up the mountain at a snail's pace. This is a point of aggravation for most people but a welcome respite for weedophiles who can use the time to see how much smoke they can fill the structure with before they get to the top. It's the perfect game: There are no losers, and everyone gets stoned.

Chronic, widely used and acceptable slang term for high-quality marijuana. Depending on who and where one is, it could refer to weed laced with cocaine or a certain strain of herb so magical and pure that one can count the crystals of THC and reddish fibers perched among its buds. Be very sure which definition the dealer subscribes to before buying chronic: One could have the best high of one's life, or quite possibly the last.

Clean, the state one attains by refraining from smoking marijuana or ingesting drugs of any kind for an extended period of time. This is occasionally done willingly as an attempt to kick an unwelcome drug habit. However, more often than not it is done begrudgingly in order to pass a drug test and secure employment or to placate nosy parental units. Thankfully, this state is not permanent.

Cigarette Joint, a form of joint that is crafted by sacrificing a perfectly sociable cigarette in order to fashion a makeshift marijuana receptacle. The smoker gently coaxes the tobacco out of the cigarette by rubbing it between the thumb and forefinger until there is nothing left but a hollow tube, which can then be filled with pot. Filling the resulting tube with weed bit by bit can be a painstaking process; however, it is a useful skill to develop for instances when one lacks more elaborate paraphernalia. Also, the resulting joint can be discreetly slipped into a pack of cigarettes where it can hide in plain sight when a stoner is attending concerts or walking around town. A pot smoker just needs to be sure to remember which one is which.

Clogged, a worrisome state for a bong or pipe, in which the chamber becomes blocked with resin, ash, and grime. As a result, smoke cannot escape and the device is transformed into an elaborate sculpture that serves no useful purpose. As hard as one might try, it is impossible to inhale a decent hit once the piece reaches this state. A poker or cleaning solution can be employed to remedy the situation, although it is far more likely that the owner will simply set the piece aside with the intention of cleaning it later and smoke out of something else. While it may appear that stoners with vast collections of bowls and bongs have a greater appreciation for the craft of piece-making than others, it is far more likely they just haven't gotten around to unclogging the first one yet.

See also **bong; Formula 420; poker (device)**

Closet Stoner, a self-loathing breed of pot smoker so ashamed of the smoking lifestyle that he or she will do everything possible to hide the habit from society. They often give no outward signs of being a stoner, shunning the characteristic long hair, laid-back attitude, and thoughtful manner of speech adopted by other breeds. When they believe no one is paying attention, however, they will quickly bust out a concealed joint, light up, take a few hits, extinguish the roach, swallow it, spray cologne or perfume, and go about their day as if nothing strange has just occurred. It is best to avoid outing closet stoners, as admitting their love of herb is a decision each closet stoner must come to on his or her own terms.

See also antisocial stoner; casual stoner; enhancement stoner; intellectual stoner; lazy stoner; paranoid stoner; quiet stoner; stoner

Coconut Bong, a bong for the true tropical island experience. Coconut bongs are beneficial in several ways. Not only do they look cool, they come with built-in bong water that helps flavor the smoke. On the downside, it's a lot of work to put into

© istockphoto / jaroon

something that's going to rot in a few days. Coconut bongs are essential for a smoker's first trip to Hawaii or Jamaica and are best used when wearing a lei and a bathing suit, and blasting "Jammin'" by Bob Marley.

See also **apple pipe**

Cold Turkey, a process of eliminating a vice from one's lifestyle that one deems undesirable, such as smoking pot. The subject, often on a whim and without warning, ceases to indulge the habit immediately. Subjects will generally delude themselves into believing it was totally their idea, although the decision is usually preceded by an ultimatum dictated by a loved one such as cutting off financial support or withholding sexual favors if the offending subject does not kick the habit. It almost never works for anybody. However, perhaps one should give it a shot anyway.

See also **clean**

Connect, the dude who provides one with pot, or the dude who sells pot to the dude who provides one with pot, or the dude whose dude sold his pot to him back in the day before he bugged out on some wack merch and started selling mood crystals near the bus stop.

Contact High, a phenomenon wherein a person not directly involved in a smoking session still exhibits many of the same symptoms and behaviors of those who are active participants. This can usually be attributed to breathing in secondhand smoke that has accumulated in a small, confined, poorly venti-lated area. Nonsmokers who inad-vertently experience a contact high, unable to make the correlation between their new surroundings and the sudden surge of eupho-ria, often subconsciously seek out groups of stoners to befriend. The level of irony in this phenomenon is directly proportional to how mor-ally opposed to marijuana use the subject claims to be.

© istockphoto / ianmcdonnell

See also hotbox

Controlled Breathing, a form of respiration utilized during a smoking session when the number of people present in a smoking cir-cle exceeds the amount of available pot necessary to get everyone high. By inhaling deeply and holding one's breath for several seconds, one can give the THC-laden smoke as much time as possible to percolate in the lungs and increase the likelihood that the desired state of baked-ness will be attained. The pot smoker just needs to remember to start breathing again after exhaling.

Cool, a versatile colloquialism whose meaning can shift depending on what circle it is being used in. For example, the general public uses it to imply that something is impressive, neat, or generally good. In pot-smoking circles these meanings still apply, but the word can also mean that somebody has been indoctrinated into the cannabis culture and is most certainly not a cop. It can also mean that somebody has had enough pot to smoke at a given moment and does not need any more. Technically the word can also mean that something is at a relatively low temperature comparative to other things, although that has absolutely nothing to do with pot and thus has little relevance in this encyclopedia.

See also **uncool**

Corner Store, a place of business that carries Twinkies, chocolate milk, tortilla chips, doughnuts, other assorted foodstuff, lottery tickets, lighters, and other impulse purchases. The corner store is a friend of the stoner as it carries everything he or she needs for the postsmoke binge. There are few things more embarrassing, though, than wandering into the corner store at 2 A.M. and slapping some frozen French bread pizza and a slushie down on the counter. The only thing inhibiting such routine embarrassment is the distance from the stoner's couch to the corner store, which, whether a mile away or a block away, always seems like an unendurable journey.

Cornering, an obscure piece of pot etiquette observed by considerate smokers to ensure that all parties involved in a session can experience the first hit of a fresh bowl. Instead of shoving the lighter nearly into the bowl head and scorching the entire cache of pot, the smoker lights only a small portion of the weed and passes it to the next person. It is a surefire way to make new friends.

See also **green hit**

Cotton Mouth, (if seeking information about the poisonous reptile because of a recent snakebite, stop flipping through an encyclopedia about marijuana and seek immediate medical attention), an unfortunate side effect of smoking marijuana wherein the mouth transforms from a moist, relatively cooperative environment to a dry, barren wasteland, thus making it nearly impossible to speak, eat, and worse, continue smoking. Effective temporary solutions include drinking large quantities of water, chewing gum, sucking on ice, or playing chubby bunny. Ineffective temporary solutions include spitting, eating saltines, and rubbing the tongue with sandpaper.

Creeper, marijuana that has a tendency to sneak up on the user. The individual will smoke a reasonable amount of pot or eat an entire brownie but not feel the effects right away. This can be especially problematic if the user attempts to remedy the situation by smoking more weed instead of waiting patiently for the high to kick in. This is a very odd evolutionary adaptation on the part of the plant, as it actually entices animals to eat more of it.

Crunked, the process of being both on chronic and drunk. High plus drunk equals crunked. The term gained widespread recognition in 1995 thanks to former *The Simpsons* writer and late-night martyr Conan O'Brien, who, along with cohost Andy Richter, used the phrase as a way to get around the censors, i.e. "That is crunked up!" Part of the story is also that Ice T, a guest on Conan's show that night, fed the late-night host the word beforehand. Southern rappers were also fond of the term, and it has since entered the pop-rap scene. Lil' Jon's song "Get Crunk" really boosted the word's use, same as his music did for the words "Yeah," "OK," and "Skeet." Apparently the censors still haven't figured out what "skeet" means.

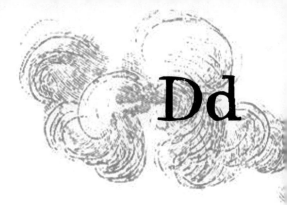

Dd

Dank, pot that has been deemed to be of especially high quality. While there are no universal criteria for grading marijuana, dank weed is generally slightly sticky to the touch, riddled with brownish-red hairs, carries a pleasantly skunky odor, and is extremely potent. Inexperienced smokers should refrain from using this term, as it is rather embarrassing to declare low-grade schwag as being "dank" simply because one lacks a basis for proper comparison.

See also **bomb; headie; ill; skunk**

Dark Alley, a narrow strip of land located between two closely placed buildings whose proximity and height blocks city lights from reaching the ground. Dark alleys are desirable locations for crime, superhero justice, police car chases, fence jumping, garbage disposal, stray cats, and marijuana smoking. The dark alley is the perfect nighttime spot for the city smoker on the go. If a police car happens to drive by, or, even worse, turn down the alley, smokers are prewired to ditch the pot and, while walking discreetly back into civilization, advise the others in the group to, "Be cool, yo, be cool."

See also **connect; dealers; drug deal; running**

Dark Side of the Rainbow, a phrase referencing the fact that when one smokes an outrageous amount of pot and listens to Pink Floyd's sixth album, *The Dark Side of the Moon*, while watching the family film *The Wizard of Oz*, certain elements of the film line up perfectly with the lyrics and tempo of the album. Sort of. This phenomenon is high-exclusive, meaning it can be observed only while under the influence of cannabis. Members of the band have repeatedly insisted the synchroniza-tion is pure coincidence, but the evidence is pretty difficult to dispute. One example includes "Eclipse," the last song on the album, concluding with the sound of a heartbeat as Dorothy puts her hand to the Tin Man's chest. There are only two possible explanations: 1) The members of Pink Floyd were so high that they synched their album to a popular children's movie and completely forgot about it, or 2) aliens, dissatisfied with the movie's original soundtrack, beamed down to the studio, directed the members of Pink Floyd to create an alternate score to their favorite film, and then erased their memories. The two are equally plausible.

See also **highdea**

Deadhead, a stoner who follows the San Francisco-based jam band The Grateful Dead, whose styles ran from electric blues to psychedelia and space rock. The band performed for thirty years before the death of guitarist Jerry Garcia. The term Deadhead reflects their fascination with the band and their current mental state. To become a Deadhead, one must consume a minimum of 100 hours of Garcia solos, smoke weed daily while wearing a tie-dye shirt and bandana, and grow one's hair down to at least nipple length. Deadheads are also required to allow at least a three-second gap between someone calling their name and them responding.

Dealers, Good Samaritans who risk fines, community service, and potential incarceration to supply the world's stoners with a steady stream of marijuana. They come from all walks of life and represent every gender, creed, and sexual orientation on the planet, so identifying one can be difficult. Some signs to look for are loose-fitting clothing, preferences for poorly lit areas, unwavering fear of and disdain for police, and ownership of a digital scale.

See also connect; drug deal; scale

Déjà Vu, the semimystical feeling that encompasses one's person that the current moment or experience has happened to the individual before, even if he or she can't place where or when exactly. Déjà vu is an oft-studied phenomenon but little understood. In pot-smoking circles, it describes the experience of hearing a stoner tell the same joke or story over multiple smoking sessions without remorse, recollection, or shame.

Dime Bag, a slang term used to describe a small plastic bag filled with approximately $10 worth of marijuana. While considered a mere pittance of pot in the current smoking society, older stoners will often reminisce that a dime bag used to be "a decent amount of weed." If left unchecked, they will also go on to describe how much better the bud they smoked back in the day was and how Woodstock "really meant something, man." The appropriate responses, in order, are: "Inflation's a bitch," "The average THC levels of marijuana were eight times higher in 2004 than they were in the '70s," and "No, it was a self-serving excuse to get high and listen to music. Not that there's anything wrong with that."

See also eighth; gram; nickel bag

Doob, a slang term for a marijuana cigarette, which is merely a shortening of another popular term, "doobie." The term is almost universally understood to be a wildly uncool way to refer to a joint. However, it is so uncool that evoking it can actually come around full circle to make one sound cool again. A similar phenomenon exists with several breeds of dogs (e.g., pugs, Mexican hairless, and Boston terriers) that go so far down the ugly spectrum that they come back around to being cute.

See also joint

Dope, a derogatory term common among teachers, parents, and police officers to refer to marijuana and various other drugs like cocaine and heroin. The term is also common in PSAs that generally involve one or more characters smoking pot, doing something stupid like climbing a water tower or playing with guns, and end with the line "There's a reason they call it dope." Anyone who has ever smoked pot, however, knows that climbing tall objects or examining firearms is on the stoner's to-do list somewhere between run a marathon and ask a police officer for directions.

Drag, a single pull of a joint or blunt that can last for as long as it has to. Subjects place the unlit end into their mouths and inhale, continuing to do so until they have had enough, a coughing fit sets in, or they pass out. Whichever comes first.

See also controlled breathing; inhale; puff; pull; toke

Drug, any chemical, plant, food, mineral, gas, or currently undiscovered substance that alters the normal function of the human body. The definition is so broad that it can literally apply to anything. A pencil, for example, if ground up and snorted would sure as hell have a negative effect on one's sense of smell and taste. Does that make it a drug? Also, if one were to smoke so much pot that being high literally became the normal state of being, would breathable air become a drug by default? And wouldn't pot then cease to be a drug for that person? Unfortunately, the folks making anti-drug laws were not nearly stoned enough during their meetings to travel down this obscure way of thinking. Otherwise, the list of illegal drugs would simply be an infinite symbol.

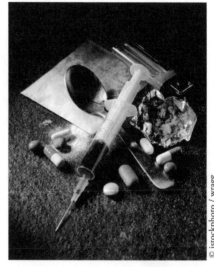

© istockphoto / wragg

Drug Deal, a scenario in which a dealer meets with a client for the purpose of exchanging some form of drug (cocaine, marijuana, heroin, PCP, etc.), for money, goods, or services. Preferably money. Because of the illegal nature of these meetings, they are usually staged in areas where it is unlikely any law enforcement agents will be in attendance, such as dark alleys, rundown apartment complexes, public bathrooms, and quiet side streets. Before participating in a drug deal, one should always ask the supposed dealer if he or she is a cop. Even if the alleged dealer is, it's possible that the person could lie and say he or she isn't. However, asking will at least provide a false sense of security.

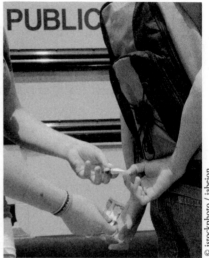

See also **connect; dealers**

Dry, an undesirable state of being wherein the subject is completely bereft of any smokable or edible marijuana and is unable to obtain any in a timely fashion. It is believed the term is derived from the expression "the well is dry," which is used to declare that a local source of water has been depleted of all its life-giving resources. However, the term could also be in reference to the state of the subject's eyes after hours of crying over a depleted stash.

See also **buzzkiller**

Dude, one of the pot smoker's four-letter words, along with cool, nice, and food. Dude is unique in English usage in that it is typically an unnecessary word that precedes an unnecessary statement. For example: "Dude, these Alpha-Bits spell 'Vengroli.'" Dude is a term currently associated with surfer culture, and it is legally prohibited from being said by anyone who shops at Eddie Bauer. However, it is routinely overused by stoners, who can conduct full conversations using only the word "dude," as Matt Stone and Trey Parker showed in the movie *BASEketball*. Dude is also used derisively by curmudgeonly antistoners trying to delegitimize what the stoner considers profound, practical insights. Sarcastically they'll say, "Yo dude, hey man, like, that's totally far out." The only proper response is to say, "Dude, weak," and immediately light up in as close proximity to the person as possible.

See also **cool**

Duffle Bag, a rectangular- or oval-shaped gym bag that can be utilized as a carry-on bag on an airplane or a makeshift briefcase in an emergency. Duffle bags are also a convenient and inconspicuous way to store large amounts of weed. While they seem convenient and can be a loyal companion for many years, they are also the No. 1 choice of the dealer who gets found out, as almost all police-bust photos involve weed overflowing from a duffle bag. Intelligent stoners know ahead of time: If their dealer uses a duffle bag, it's best to find another dealer.

See also dealers

Dugout, a case used for storing marijuana containing a small chamber to house the pot and another compartment just large enough for a one-hitter, affectionately referred to as the "bat." This piece of paraphernalia is ideal for the pothead on the go, because it allows a smoker to discreetly pack a bowl, take a hit, and disappear like a ninja in a cloud of smoke long before bystanders even realize what's happened.

See also one-hitter

Durban Poison, a highly potent strain of marijuana grown in the very hot regions of South Africa, including the coastal area of Kwa-Zulu-Natal. The bud smells like candy and is about as common there, especially in the city where it gets its namesake. Pot tourists travel to the country for the strain specifically where they acquire it from black market pushers on the streets; the drug remains technically illegal there despite its widespread use. It's no surprise the Zulu people consider themselves "people of heaven," as they surround themselves with vast swaths of untouched weed, which is what most weedheads consider heaven to be anyway.

Dusting, the act of sprinkling any number of illicit substances such as cocaine, heroin, or PCP into a joint, blunt, bowl, or bong before smoking. It is considered extremely poor form to attempt this without first consulting everyone else in the group, as not all smokers are comfortable expanding their horizons beyond humble cannabis. Some people deem it an unnecessary practice, likening it to topping a delicious cheese pizza with salty, slimy sardines. Why ruin a good thing?

Dutch Master, an inexpensive brand of cigar, the contents of which are commonly discarded so they can be replaced with a far superior filling: marijuana. The flavor profile and distinct aroma of an unaltered Dutch Master have been documented only in lab settings, as no member of the general public has ever smoked one without some degree of enhancement.

See also **blunt**

Easy Rider, a marijuana variety designed to be as easy to grow as it is to smoke. A hybrid strain of part sativa and part indica, Easy Rider can be grown indoors or out, by experienced growers or novices. It grows to about two feet tall and has about a 12 to 15 percent THC level, making it ideal for clandestine, high-yield pot growing.

See also hybrid

Eating the Peanut, a ritual performed in some smoking circles in which the person holding the joint when it becomes too small to be smoked without risking injury plops it into his or her mouth and swallows it. Waste not, want not. This practice is also observed during unexpected encounters with police officers, although it is not called eating the peanut. Under those circumstances it is merely called common sense.

Eighth, denomination in which marijuana is generally sold, in reference to an eighth of an ounce. Eighths cost anywhere from $30 to $70, depending on the grade of weed, geographic location, and general weed climate. As the well dries up, prices rise. Supply-and-demand economics. Eighths of pot last about a month when not properly stored before the plant begins to dry out and the grade drops, leading many smokers to exclaim, "We gotta smoke it before it goes bad!" This leads to more eighths purchases, which in turn leads to more weed smoking, and the vicious, beautiful cycle continues forever.

See also **gram; ounce**

Emotional stoner, a person who has taken one too many hits. Because emotions are accentuated when stoned, it's not uncommon for an emotional stoner to tell those in the smoking circle he or she loves them all. Do not attempt to restrain these stoners. They will soon feel such shame for their showy display of affection that they will begin to cry. The shame will be compounded to such a degree that they will leave the room, and the problem will have taken care of itself.

See also **active stoner; antisocial stoner; artistic stoner; enhancement stoner; social stoner; stoner; talkative stoner**

Enhancement Stoner, a breed of stoner succinctly portrayed by comedian Jon Stewart in the stoner film *Half Baked*. Enhancement stoners have convinced themselves that every activity is infinitely better after one has consumed marijuana. To them, going to the zoo is okay, but going to the zoo on weed is simply a much more worthwhile adventure. A little toke here and there to liven up certain activities is fine. However, if the response when asked if one would like to go smoke a joint is, "Hold on, let me smoke a bowl first," one might have crossed the line into enhancement stoner territory.

See also **active stoner; antisocial stoner; artistic stoner; social stoner; stoner; talkative stoner**

Euphemisms, the use of more polite-sounding words or phrases to describe things that are undesirable or better left unsaid. Examples include: "hooked up," "in between jobs," "big-boned," etc. Clever stoners employ euphemisms when they run into authority figures in the hopes that they can elicit laughter amongst their friends while keeping the fact that they're stoned quiet. The response to a question like "Are you high?" could result in the following euphemism: "No, we were just bobbin' the Marley." The authority figure will respond "What?" and the stoner will say, "You know, just exploring the atmosphere, suckin' the succor, puffin' the magic dragon." Upon completion of this sentence, the stoner will flash an ear-to-ear smile at his friends, who will have missed it because they've already started running.

Euphoria, a state of general contentedness which can be achieved through positive thinking, proper diet, and meditation. Or one can take a shortcut and smoke pot. When in this state, one feels on top of the world, as if absolutely nothing could possibly go wrong. This is usually followed by something going wrong, such as an unexpected encounter with law enforcement. Once the dust has settled, this often results in the subject smoking additional pot to get back to the euphoric state, only to be brought down again by another issue. Some call this addiction. Others call it Thursday.

Euro Style, a method for consuming marijuana wherein smokers take several long hits until they are satisfied with the amount they have smoked before passing it to the next person. This method runs contrary to the regimented style employed in the United States, during which participants take precisely two hits before passing the smoking apparatus to their neighbor. When smoking Euro style, one should adhere to the self-imposed rules one might follow at an all-you-can-eat buffet. Just because one is allowed to eat seven plates of crab cakes in a single sitting does not mean that one should.

See also **puff, puff, pass**

Exhaling, the means by which smoke that has been inhaled into the lungs can be expelled from the body. This exercise should be attempted only once the smoke has had a chance to permeate the lungs and harness the THC's mind-altering powers. If one is so stoned that one forgets to perform this necessary maneuver, never fear—one's body will figure it out in due time.

See also **inhaling**

Ff

Fake Inhale, a sneaky trick employed by individuals who do not actually want to smoke pot but still want to fit in with their social group. When it is their turn to take a hit, they will take the smoke into their mouths similar to their friends, but they will not actually inhale the smoke. Instead, they will merely open their mouths and expel the smoke, giving the appearance that they have inhaled. Not only is this an embarrassing display that is unlikely to fool anyone, it is also a waste of perfectly good weed.

See also inhale

Fatty, a large, plump, delectable marijuana cigarette. A fatty is rolled with 100 percent all-natural marijuana and should never contain additives like tobacco, cocaine, or PCP. The term can also be used to describe a particularly large, plump, delectable ass belonging to an equally large, plump, and delectable human, so it is important to take note of one's surroundings before exclaiming, "Yo, let me tap that fatty." Depending on the context, doing so could result in a satisfying hit from a joint or an unsatisfying punch in the face.

See also joint

Fiending, a state of being characterized by an extreme desire to locate, purchase, and smoke some form of marijuana. Headies, mids, schwag—it doesn't matter. While studies have shown that marijuana is not physically addictive, stoners who have been unable to obtain smokable weed during an extended period of time will often exhibit symptoms such as irritability, anxiety, depression, and an insatiable desire to search their rooms for misplaced ganja. The only known cure for this ailment is 100 CCs of weed—stat.

Fire, an extremely hot entity created when a substance in an oxygen-rich environment is heated to a given temperature known as its flash point. It is an essential ingredient in the equation "marijuana plus fire equals high." Fire can easily be created with the help of a lighter or matches, although stoners have been known to employ kitchen stoves when necessary. When safely controlled, fire can be more entertaining to a stoner than music, television, and philosophy combined.

Five-O, a slang term derived from the cop series *Hawaii Five-O,* used to describe the po-po, pigs, fuzz, cops, and police. It remains one of the most enduring, culturally relevant aspects of the show. Five-O is the natural enemy of the marijuana smoker, like a wolf to the stoner's sheep, and can be uniformed or undercover. A simple, sudden "Five-O! Five-O!" in stoner language means put the blunt out, toss the baggie and run, or eat the weed. It is for this reason that one should never carry more pot than one can eat.

© istockphoto / jodiecoston

Foil Pipe, an inexpensive homemade smoking device consisting entirely of aluminum foil. Fledgling stoners too young to procure a legit pipe or desperate potheads who have misplaced their favorite piece can quickly craft this tool with the aid of a pen, marker, or other cylindrical object and a sheet of foil. While it scores very low on aesthetics and usability, it scores very high on disposability, as it can be balled up and discarded in a matter of seconds if the smoking session is compromised.

See also **apple pipe; highlighter pipe**

Forget Me Now, a special pill that creates a temporary forgetfulness in humans. It is a mainstay of the magician's toolkit to be used in case a magician accidentally reveals the secret of his trick. While its effects are identical to the drug Rohypnol, any similarities are coincidental. Stoners generally have little use for the pill, as marijuana is a natural forget me now in its own right.

Formula 420, any cleaning products that can be used to remove tar, resin, ash, odor, and general griminess that can accumulate inside of

anything used for smoking pot. Simply pour the solution into the piece, cover the openings, shake for one minute, and rinse to restore the paraphernalia to a state similar to how it looked before it contained more resin than glass.

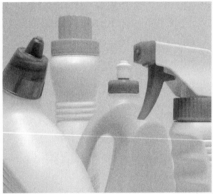

© istockphoto / YvanDube

See also stoke

Fourthmeal, a concept that was part of a 2006 advertising campaign launched by the fast-food restaurant Taco Bell. Clearly aimed exclusively at midnight tokers, the term describes an eating experience between the hours of dinner and breakfast that often begins with harmless conventional snacking but quickly escalates to include larger items like tacos, burritos, and quesadillas. In a shocking coincidence, all of the food items associated with fourthmeal can be found on Taco Bell's menu, allowing the chain to completely monopolize an entire meal.

See also midnight toker

Free-Range Weed, a term used to refer to pot that has been planted in a secluded stretch of forest, an unused trail in a local park, or an unused plot in a community garden and left to grow on its own without the aid of fertilizer, artificial sunlight, or pesticides. This hands-off style of farming offers all the benefits of growing one's own pot with far less risk of legal ramifications. While it may be impossible to prevent thieves from pilfering the budding plants, at least the grower has plausible deniability should anyone start wondering why the local rabbit population has suddenly taken to rolling on their backs and staring at the clouds for hours at a time.

French Inhale, a parlor trick wherein smoke is released from the mouth and simultaneously inhaled through the nose, creating an unbroken chain of smoke. Although there is little to no practical application of the technique, it is very popular at parties and will often elicit godlike reverence from onlookers who have not yet figured out how to perform the maneuver themselves. The far less impressive Norwegian inhale, in which the smoker exhales into a jar and seals the lid for later use, has yet to catch on.

Fried, a state of complete and utter bakedness. The subject is so high, he or she can do little more than slump over on the couch and stare off into space while occasionally eating a few Oreos. While the subject could be contemplating very deep, thought-provoking concepts, it is far more likely that he or she is simply wondering if it's possible to overdose on marijuana.

See also **baked; half-baked; high; stoned; wasted**

Friends, individuals with whom one generally associates, shares common interests, and likes. Friends are broken down into three categories: 1) Best friends 2) General friends 3) Frienemies. The definitions are distinct in the pot world. For example, frienemies are those friends who always leech off one's weed supply. General friends are those with whom one will frequently get high. And best friends are the ones who, when one is craving a joint at a party, pull one out of a back pocket, along with a lighter. All three inhabit a smoker's world at any given moment, and it's certain that the best friend will be a best man or bridesmaid at the wedding. Everyone else gets usher status.

Full Moon Party, the international smoker's haven for all things beach, party, and beach party. Held on the beautiful and crowded beaches of the town of Hat Rin on the Thai island of Ko Pha-ngan, the Full Moon Party happens once each month when the moon is full (go figure). The rager attracts stoners from around the world for its infamous buckets of booze, fire dancers, and tasty Thai herb. Haad Rin beach bars stay open all night to serve the 20,000–30,000 Full Moon Partiers, who dance to drum and bass, house, and reggae music—and smoke till sunrise. Attendees don't have to speak Thai, but it helps if they know what a Thai stick is.

See also **Thai stick**

Funny Before Feelings, an understanding reached among members of the smoking community that the mental well-being of any individual is secondary to saying something the rest of the group will find amusing, at least while everyone in a group is stoned. This philosophy is not universally understood, however, so it is best to test the waters with a minor put-down before graduating to "your mama" jokes and accusations of bed-wetting.

© istockphoto / RyanJLane

Gg

G-13, a strain of pot of such urban legend it may have been briefly considered as the subject of an Indiana Jones movie. Allegedly, the U.S. government genetically engineered G-13 while developing strains of marijuana at the University of Mississippi in the 1970s. Its THC level apparently reaches 28 percent, which is among the highest of any known strand. There's no evidence to support the claims that G-13 exists, but dealers who want to earn an extra buck on an eighth may claim to have the G-13 stuff, and smokers who want to think they're smoking G-13 may knowingly go along with the ruse.

Ganja, the Sanskrit word for hemp which has been adapted by English-speaking pot smokers as another slang term for the drug. The word is more typically used in West Indian countries. When being spoken in America, it works most aptly with a crowd listening to reggae music or anything with a sitar.

Gateway Drug, term used to describe marijuana by the antidrug crowd amongst a larger argument about the ill effects of legalizing or decriminalizing the herb. The idea is that marijuana, while not harmful in and of itself, is the first drug users will take en route to more dangerous drugs. The argument is propagated by the news, talk show guests, eighth-grade health teachers, and concerned parents. It is an argument that has been largely debunked by scientific evaluation. A twelve-year University of Pittsburgh study found that any number of sequences can take place regarding where marijuana falls in a user's drug progression, and none of them indicate whether a user will move on to stronger drugs. Welcome relief for pot smokers, but terrible news for heroin dealers.

Gazebo, a small wooden structure located in many gardens and parks. Even though they are usually completely open to the elements, they do offer modest cover from prying eyes, which makes them popular smoker hangouts for young stoners who don't have the luxuries of apartments or cars to retreat to for their sessions. Luckily, police officers can see a stoner only if he or she moves, so those smoking in gazebos can evade them by remaining motionless.

See also **park**

Generation Joint, a marijuana cigarette that has been imbued with the concentrated potency of five or six older joints that have been reduced to roaches. Once the generation joint has been smoked to near completion, it can then be saved for later use as the base for a third-generation joint, several of which can then be saved up for a fourth-generation joint, and so on. In order to create a ninth-generation joint, one would need to first create 1,953,125 roaches. Better get started.

See also **roach**

Ghost Hit, a rare phenomenon where, during the course of a smoking session, one of the participants manages to hold in a single hit of marijuana for so long that little to no visible smoke escapes when he or she exhales. To the untrained eye it may appear as if the subject has not actually inhaled any smoke at all. This is not the case, however. In truth, the smoke has merely been absorbed by the body or is temporarily trapped behind a pocket of bong resin that has built up in the lungs. There is the slight possibility that an actual ghost has possessed the body of the subject and taken the hit for himself. This possibility is especially troubling, as it would indicate that all of the wonders of the afterlife and benefits of complete spiritual enlightenment still pale in comparison to a single bong rip.

God Bud, a strain of marijuana that is intoxicatingly delicious and perhaps the first and most popular use of marketing in advertising when it comes to strains. God bud is a great, award-winning strain. It is dense, the high is very satisfying, and it has one of the most alluring names in all of weed. Anyone who hears the name "God bud" wants that stuff immediately—even atheists.

Google, the most powerful and precise search engine, as well as a mail, map, directions, recipe service, news aggregator, and one-stop shop for most everything on the Internet. Google has helped users find the most obscure and hard-to-find information, and it is theorized that Google contains every bit of knowledge available. If the meaning of life exists, it is likely stored somewhere on Google. With such endless information, Google is a key partner for all sorts of stoner activities. Not only is finding stoner message boards a cinch, Google searches can also yield practical pot-related advice: how to plant seeds, where to buy seeds, how to roll a joint, fun things to do while high, fun places to pass out while high, food to eat while high, things to tell police while high, things to tell the judge while

© istockphoto / ssuni

high, things to tell one's cellmates while high, things to tell the parole officer while high. . . .

Gram, a unit of mass in the metric system defined as the weight of one cubic centimeter of water. The gram is also a standard unit of measure in the world of marijuana, and 3½ grams equals ⅛ of an ounce is the standard conversion between the metric and English marijuana systems. Grams of weed generally cost between $15 to $20 and can be reserved for either stoners who want higher-grade stuff to keep costs low or the less-consistent smoker to keep the weed fresh. Grams can usually provide for two to three joints, or about ten small bowls, which for some is about one day's supply.

Grass (plant), a slang term for marijuana likely stemming from the mild similarities in color and appearance between graminoids, the most prevalent plant on earth, and cannabis sativa, the most prevalent plant in college dorm rooms. It is very important to avoid using this term unless both parties are aware of its double meaning. For example, it could be very disappointing for a sheepherder to be led to a remote location expecting to find fields of food for his sheep only to discover a bag of mind-altering drugs. Although, perhaps not.

Gravity Bong, a variety of smoking device, usually homemade, that consists of a plastic jug or bottle with the bottom removed and a bowl head inserted into the cap. The makeshift bong is then inserted into a tub of water, marijuana is placed into the bowl and lit, and the bong is slowly drawn upward to pull smoke inside. Finally, the cap is unscrewed and the smoker places his or her mouth over the opening and pushes the bong back down, rapidly filling the lungs to capacity with an intense hit of smoke. The existence of the gravity bong is indisputable evidence that smokers are far more intelligent and inventive than one could ever possibly imagine.

See also apple pipe; bong; foil pipe; highlighter pipe

Green, one of the three primary colors that can be seen in American money, leprechauns, and various forms of vegetation, most notably marijuana. The term has been adopted by the pot-smoking community as a euphemism both for the drug itself as well as for money, which coincidentally can be used to purchase more weed.

Green Dragon, The, a drink made when mixing vodka and marijuana. When boiling bud in some vodka, a green liquid will form, thus creating a not-so-tasty drink that will get stoners high as a kite and drunk as a hobo, all at the same time. Obviously the best way to get crunk, it is best to strain all weed out of the vodka before imbibing to create a smooth and pleasurable experience. In an unrelated note, this is also the name of the best bar in all of Middle Earth.

Green Hit, the first hit of a freshly packed bowl of marijuana, so named because the color of the weed has not yet turned an ashen gray. Marijuana connoisseurs prize the first hit due to its crisp, clean flavor. It is considered good etiquette to offer it to other members of the circle when packing a bowl. Tragically, it is also considered good etiquette not to be greedy and accept the green hit for oneself, thus creating a never-ending cycle of generous offers and respectful declinations that can carry on for anywhere from several awkward seconds to several awkward hours before somebody finally caves.

See also **cornering**

Green Leafy Substance, a euphemism employed by various law enforcement agencies and journalists to refer to any piece of plant matter that is most certainly marijuana but cannot be referred to as such until a battery of tests can be performed to confirm the obvious. Its use perpetuates the absurd belief that there are actually groups of people in the world who walk around the streets carrying baggies of oregano in the event they get a hankering for pizza and, alas, the restaurant is fresh out.

See also **cannabis**

Grinder, a circular contraption that consists of two interlocking hollow halves with small protrusions sticking out from the inside of each half. It is an essential tool when rolling joints, as it does exactly what its name implies—it grinds. One places pot in between the two halves, closes them together, and twists in opposing directions to transform large nugs into a relatively uniform consistency that burns more evenly. One could also use scissors or one's hands for this purpose, but studies have shown the grinder to be at least six times more fun.

Hh

H.R. Pufnstuf, a 1970s children's entertainment program whose multiple marijuana references subliminally raised a generation of unknowing soon-to-be pot smokers. While the producers deny the program had any intentional references to drugs, the evidence is pretty overwhelming. The show's plot involves a young boy trapped on an island in which the imagery is multicolored and psychedelic, and every plant and animal can talk. Also, the title character often used phrases like "Whoa, dude," or "Far out," which any Five-O knows only comes out of the mouths of stoners. Theories are that *H.R. Pufnstuf* is short for hand-rolled puffin' stuff. The producers also later produced a show called *Lidsville*. "Lid" was 1970s slang for an ounce of marijuana. Also, just, come on.

Hacky Sack, a specific brand of footbag that has become synonymous with the "sport" played by pot-smoking hippies as early as the 1950s. The game consists of two or more players standing in a circle moving the bean-filled bag from person to person without the use of their hands and without allowing it to touch the ground. As far as anyone can tell, there is no time limit, no means of keeping score, and no way to win. It is literally the ideal stoner game, as one's enjoyment has absolutely nothing to do with how good one is at it.

Half-Baked, a state of being for stoners wherein one is not completely high but most certainly at least a little buzzed. It gets its name from a half-baked cookie, which is still a little soft and gooey on the inside, which is how a half-baked stoner would describe him or herself as feeling. Similar to the cookie, the stoner need but fire up the oven (read: light joint) in order to reach the proper level of bakedness.

See also **baked; high**

Handy Stoner, a type of smoker who is capable of building paraphernalia with nearly any combination of items. Need to smoke in an open field with only a plastic bag, a car battery, and a hunting knife? He's got it covered.

See also **active stoner; intellectual stoner; social stoner; stoner; talkative stoner**

Hash Bar, a term used to refer to a coffeehouse in the Netherlands where it is perfectly legal to buy, sell, and consume marijuana in small quantities. In other words, stoner heaven. Cannabis purchased from these locales is generally of a higher quality than that purchased on the street, and because they are not technically illegal they attract visitors from all across the world searching for a way to get high without having to buy pot from a shady character in a dark alley. The laws surrounding the coffeeshops (apparently spelling it as one word eliminates the possibility of confusion with a traditional coffee shop) can be extremely confusing and contradictory at times. For example, it is legal to sell marijuana there, but it is not necessarily legal for the shop to buy pot to sell to customers. Also, the coffeeshops are technically not allowed to advertise their status as purveyors of pot, but the billowing smoke coming from the exits is generally a dead giveaway.

Hash Bash, an annual gathering in early April of stoners on the University of Michigan campus. The purpose is generally to oppose state marijuana laws, even though Michigan has some of the most lenient laws in America and Ann Arbor has decriminalized the drug. The event culminates at high noon, when students gather around the Quad and sit around stoned, which is called the "Hour of Power." Hash Bash organizers warn students to pregame and not to get high at the event, as cops can bust for possession. Still, students are encouraged to get high off-campus, where the fine is $100 or less, making Hash Bash day just like every other day, only with speakers and entertainment.

Hashish, a processed form of marijuana that takes all the best, most potent parts of the cannabis plant, shaves them off, compresses them, and creates a new sort of supermarijuana. Hashish is made up mostly of trichomes, which are fine hairlike appendages that grow off the plant and are rich in THC. Through various heating and cooling methods, the resin from the plant's trichomes is bricked and solidified. Essentially hashish is like slicing only the frosting off the best cakes and putting it together to make one super frosting-only cake, which incidentally makes a great companion to any hash-smoking experience.

See also **kief; trichomes**

Head Shop, a store where one can purchase an assortment of smoking paraphernalia ranging from simple rolling papers and pipes to more elaborate bongs, hookahs, and vaporizers. In the United States, the legality of such establishments falls into a hazy gray area, as many of the products they carry can be sold only for use with tobacco products or other legal herbal products. However, the vast majority of customers purchase them exclusively for use with illegal substances. This paradox necessitates a pathetic song-and-dance routine between the customer and salesperson wherein both are perfectly aware what the products are actually used for, but the two of them must act as if they have never even heard of a substance called marijuana, let alone the fact that it can be smoked out of one of the intricate structures on display. For many, their efforts to legalize marijuana are based solely on the desire to end these embarrassing displays permanently.

Headie, top-quality bud with the ability to give smokers a "heady" high. What's a "heady" high? No one can be sure, of course, as all experience is purely subjective and prone to individual interpretation. Plus its effects are so unique to each individual that some headies to one person can be something completely different to someone else. And how can it even be known that smokers get high? Maybe the sober state is really being high and being high is really being sober? How can people even know they exist anyway? Does anyone else feel a huge déjà vu feeling right now? Yeah, that's what headies do.

See also **mids; schwag**

Hemp, a jack-of-all-trades plant whose industrial uses include food, medicine, water purification, and fuel, and whose recreational purposes include getting really stoned. The difference between industrial hemp and recreational hemp is subtle

Hemp(*Cannabis sativa*). 1, 2 Flowering shoots, 1 of Staminate, 2 of Pistillate Plant ; 3 Staminate Flower ; 4 Pistillate Flower ; 5 Fruit.

but profound. For example, industrial hemp's THC content is about 0.05 percent, whereas marijuana contains anywhere from 5 to 20 percent THC levels on average. This means it would require about twenty tightly rolled joints of industrial hemp smoked in a very short period of time to experience even a mild high. This sad fact leaves many desperate smokers disappointed when, during extended weed droughts, they attempt to smoke hemp pants, leaving them both nauseous and pantsless.

Henry, an obscure piece of pot slang that requires an absurd series of mental leaps and a general understanding of world history in order to comprehend. See, Henry is short for Henry VIII, an English monarch who ruled the country from 1491–1547. The V in his name is actually the Roman numeral for five, and each I is the Roman numeral for the number one. Add them together and one gets eight, or eighth. This in turn is a universal pot term representing ⅛th of an ounce of marijuana. So, in theory, asking somebody for a Henry is equivalent to asking somebody for an eighth of weed. Please never use this slang.

Henry VIII.

Herb, a slang term for marijuana likely stemming from its resemblance, especially when ground, to various kitchen staples like basil, parsley, oregano, and thyme. To the untrained eye, marijuana is so similar to various herbs that many stoner newbs will fall for a common bait-and-switch con in which an unscrupulous dealer sells them a bag partially or entirely filled with dried herbs instead of pot. If presented with this problem, the best solution is to suck it up, smoke the oregano, pretend to experience the greatest high imaginable, and hope nobody else notices.

High, a state of sublime, subconscious self-awareness induced by smoking or otherwise consuming marijuana. While attempts to describe what it feels like to be high are varied and incomplete, some descriptions can help peel away the mystery. Some stoners claim it's like one's mind is flying. Others, while high, say it's like floating in space. Others say it's a state of pure contentedness that makes music, TV, food, sex, friends, conversation, and everything else around the smoker better. In SAT parlance:

> Getting high :: one's brain
> Eating spinach :: Popeye

See also **every entry in this book**

Highdea, a groundbreaking, earth-shattering idea, the awesomeness of which is eclipsed only by its monumental lack of any practical application. Some examples include the recliner with a built-in toilet, Da Vinci's Aerial Screw (nonfunctioning helicopter), and fourthmeal. The term can also be attributed more generally to any moment of inspiration one is struck with while under the influence of marijuana that requires the clarifying statement, "Well it sounded like a good idea when I was stoned."

Highlighter Pipe, a common writing utensil used to point out particularly important passages in books, magazines, newspapers, and legal documents that has been modified for the purpose of smoking marijuana. The device is created by removing the bottom of a highlighter, crafting a bowl out of tinfoil to push inside of the opening, and drilling a small hole into the cap to allow the user to pull the smoke out. This method is common among middle school and high school students due to the abundance of highlighters, the need for inconspicuous smoking utensils, and an inexplicable desire to make pipes out of really weird shit.

See also apple pipe; foil pipe; gravity bong

High School, a building that houses some of the most volatile, sexually charged, drug-soaked individuals on the planet—teenagers. Many young people have already dabbled with marijuana in middle school, but high school is the time when most stoners first take up the pursuit in earnest. This is not surprising, as the constant fear of rejection and sporadic ridicule associated with high school make finding a means of temporary escape not only appealing, but necessary.

Hippies, members of a subculture that emerged in the 1960s largely around the use of marijuana and LSD. Hippies were instrumental in Woodstock, the sexual revolution, the civil rights movement, and protesting the war. Though the Vietnam War ended more than three decades ago and there is no draft, hippies remain a vibrant part of most college campuses. Modern hippies have embraced a lifestyle that revolves around long hair, ponchos, sandals, acoustic guitars, sing-alongs, Eastern religions, and anticorporatism. They are mostly a derided and disrespected group, though they remain firmly committed to their legitimacy and sincerity. This commitment lasts until about three months after graduation, when hippies realize they need to cut their hair, buy a suit

© istockphoto / djgunner

not made from hemp, and land a job if they're ever going to move out of their parents' basement.

Hipsters, urban, middle-class young adults whose primary interests reside outside of mainstream culture, including but not limited to: alternative music, Thai food, thrift-store finds, Whole Foods, hand-rolled cigarettes, messenger bags, Chuck Taylors, piercings, incorporating one's nipples into a tattoo, PBR, hoodies, veganism, and of course smoking pot. Hipsters have set up armies in three American locations: Cambridge, Massachusetts; San Francisco, California; and Portland, Oregon, where they are sitting, getting high, listening to John Cage music, and planning a ground offensive for December 21, 2012, from the coasts moving inward in an effort to take over the country. The effort will fail when they get distracted to go to the next Pitchfork music festival.

Hit, a subjective slang term used by pot smokers to describe a single serving of marijuana inhaled from a joint, bowl, pipe, bong, vaporizer, hookah, or modified common household object. A hit is generally understood as a single inhalation. However, variations in lung capacity, tolerance to smoke, and overall level of selfishness vary from stoner to stoner, making it nearly impossible to set a universal definition for the term.

See also **drag; puff; pull; toke**

Holding It for a Friend, what everyone in possession of marijuana is doing, until they smoke it.

See also **sculpture**

Hoodie, a garment of cotton clothing worn on the upper body with long sleeves; a heavy, insulated fabric; a hood; and a general feeling of warmth and comfort. Hoodies are a frequent clothing choice of stoners, though the reasons remain mysterious. Some theories: Body temperature drops while stoned, and hoodies help stoners maintain a proper warmth level; the pouch that often accompanies hoodies can be used to store bowls, baggies, joints, or lighters; and perhaps most importantly, because all the cool stoners are wearing them.

© istockphoto / GaryAlvis

Hookah, a large, elaborate structure used to smoke tobacco that can also be employed for use with marijuana. The contraption consists of a base filled with water to cool the smoke, a bowl to house the tobacco, and a hose from which to pull the smoke. Many hookahs come with several hoses attached to the base, allowing multiple smokers to enjoy the experience simultaneously. This can cause immense confusion among smokers trained in the puff, puff, pass method of smoking, and it is not uncommon for first-time users to pass out from the sheer joy of being able to smoke to their heart's content without interruption.

Hot Knifing, a desperate but effective means of smoking weed when there are no other smoking devices or the marijuana level is so low its potential must be fully maximized. Hot knifing works by heating the tips of two butter knives on a stove, picking up weed as one would with chopsticks, and squeezing down on the marijuana to burn it. The smoker then uses some contraption, generally a two-liter soda bottle sliced in half, to trap and breathe in the smoke that forms. When done skillfully, the smoking experience is similar to using a vaporizer and can get smokers perfectly stoned with very little weed. It also leaves users with a set of black-tipped knives, which can be used for very little else besides more hot knifing.

Hotbox, a recreational activity wherein a group of stoners enter a confined space, light up, and recycle the air among themselves so as not to waste any precious THC-laden smoke. Common locales include bathrooms, automobiles, refrigerator boxes, dorm rooms, abandoned train cars, and large closets. Small closets would theoretically work best, but the risk of death slightly outweighs the enhancement to the smoking experience. Slightly.

See also **contact high**

Hungry Stoner, a breed of pot enthusiast completely at the mercy of food. In general, they like to have a stockpile of all the munchies they plan to consume before smoking commences. As there is no telling what foodstuffs they will find appealing after a session, they often pick several varieties from every major stoner food group: salty, sweet, deep-fried, sour, frozen, and Slurpee. Once stoned, they will devour anything and everything that is not tied down, even some things that aren't technically food (like sugar cubes). Because of this, they are invited into very few private homes.

See also **antisocial stoner; lazy stoner; paranoid stoner; quiet stoner; social stoner; stoner**

Hybrid, a cannabis plant bred using parents from two different strains. In the same way that one can, say, breed a lion with an eagle to make a griffin, different types of cannabis plants can be strategically crossbred to create new strains of marijuana that boast different traits of the parents. Hybrids can be created from either two different types of cannabis plants (e.g., a sativa/indica hybrid) or from two different strains of the same type of plant (e.g., indica/indica hybrid). Sometimes, hybrids are created in order to increase harvest productivity, as crossing a fast-growing indica plant with a slower-growing sativa plant will yield a moderately fast-growing hybrid plant. Other times, hybrids are created to produce varying types of highs. Carmelicious, for example, an indica/sativa hybrid, boasts a light, consistent, headier high, whereas Big Bud, another indica/sativa hybrid, offers a TKO time-loss-go-to-hypnotic-regression-therapy-in-an-attempt-to-recover-alien-probe-memories high.

See also **indica; sativa**

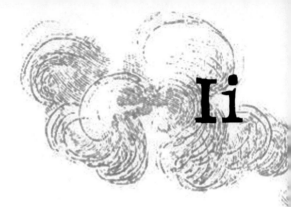

Ii

Ice, a strain of marijuana that ranks among the most potent in America and the most artistic-looking as well. Seeing ice strains makes it easy to understand where the name came from. It looks like those fine, untouched icicles in that *Planet Earth* episode "Caves." Ice pot has tentacles and fuzzy white trichomes pointing out of it, giving it a light greenish-white hue. It looks as if it was grown in a snow globe and makes the pot look angelic and innocent. As consumers quickly discover, the strain is neither.

Ice Cold, that which is cooler than being cool.

Ice Cream Shop, a store that sells marijuana. Oh yeah, it also sells ice cream. There are some places where one would pay more for a product than others. For example, one wouldn't normally pay $15 for a hot dog and beer, but if one is at a baseball game, one might. Economists call this a "fucking rip-off," but they also call it a "captive market." In this example, one is totally stoned and willing to pay $4 for a scoop of ice cream plus another \$2 to throw some crushed Snickers on top. Behind the counter at the local ice cream store, a community college dropout is happy to sell one a scoop of Chunky Monkey. But he really wants one to come into the backroom so he can sell one an eighth of Super Skunk. Just don't forget to order some ice cream before leaving. With Snickers.

Ice Hits, an elaborate method of smoking marijuana in which the smoker chills a mug in the freezer for several hours, takes a hit, exhales into the bottom of the cup, lets it sit there for a moment, shows off the display to his or her friends, and then "drinks" the smoke from the mug. Its existence is further evidence that, despite all evidence, pot smokers are some of the most ambitious members of society. They simply refuse to put their knowledge to good use and stop brainstorming new, wildly impractical yet indisputably awesome ways to get high.

Idea Book, a blank notebook kept in a stoner's apartment on the lower level of the coffee table alongside a pen. The idea book is kept within reach in case an idea or worthwhile thought occurs to the person while under the influence. These ideas are usually not worthy of writing down, as they can often include wayward movie plots or seemingly hilarious albeit completely nonsensical practical jokes that probably go over the line into the realm of illegality. Still, the idea book has value in itself, in that it tracks the story of stonerdom in whatever apartment the book happens to reside. It is also a reference tool for the bet that inevitably takes place between stoner friends: Which member of the group gets stupider when they get high? There is never a winner in such an argument.

See also highdea

Ill, a term which is widely used among the pot-smoking community to refer to anything that possesses the quality of being really, really awesome. This stands in direct opposition to the traditional definition of the word, which is used in the medical community to denote a patient who is suffering from some sort of malady and is thus not well. This phenomenon can be found elsewhere in stoner vernacular with words like "bad" (awesome), "wicked" (awesome), and "dope" (awesome). As it turns out, marijuana has a unique ability to allow the definition of any word to be temporarily changed to "awesome."

Illegal Smile, euphemism for having made a day brighter by taking a hit. The term comes from the song of the same name written and performed by country music singer John Prine. The song begins with a character whose day is going so

© istockphoto / aluxum

poorly he loses a staring contest to his bowl of oatmeal. Then something happens that is not explained, and he is suddenly wearing an "illegal smile" and things begin looking up. While it is not revealed precisely what caused the change in mood, whatever it was is fairly inexpensive, lasts quite some time, and leaves the character hiding in a closet wondering if the cops can hear his thoughts. Someday perhaps musicians will be able to stop hiding behind euphemisms and Prine will officially be able to change the name of the song to "My Day Really Sucked, So I Smoked Some Pot and Now It's Awesome."

In Plain Sight, the ideal location to hide illicit substances such as marijuana. This is not to say that one should simply leave it lying around. However, one should not waste his or her time sneaking through ventilation ducts, hollowing out the leg of a table, or prying up floorboards in an attempt to find the ideal hiding place. As far as a police officer is concerned, the most likely place for pot to be is counterintuitively the least likely place. Instead, slide it into a box set of the series *Friends*, inside of a soda can, or simply at the bottom of a tissue box. KISS: Keep it Simple, Stupid.

See also **stash can**

Incense, an organic substance that, when lit, gives off what some describe as a pleasant, soothing odor or what others describe as smelling like a flaming bag of dog shit. It is commonly employed in religious ceremonies and by high school students attempting to mask the smell of a recent pot-smoking session. When using incense for the latter purpose, one must weigh the benefits of masking the odor of skunky weed with the risk of one's room smelling like a combination of gasoline and burnt hair.

© istockphoto / 77DZIGN

Increased Attention Span, one of the side effects of smoking marijuana that appears beneficial at first but can actually be rather troublesome in practice. It's all well and good when one is able to smoke a joint and watch the entire *Lord of the Rings* trilogy without stopping. However, when there is nothing specific to pay attention to, the stoner can become confused and disoriented. For example, imagine what might happen if one were to get high, enter a toy store, and pick up a kaleidoscope. An entire day could go by before one even realized he or she was still in the store.

Indica, one of the two meta-categorizations for marijuana, along with sativa. Indica is a slightly different type of plant, however. Its leaves are shorter and stubbier than sativa, and its consumption leaves smokers in more of a lethargy than sativa. Indica is also noted for not being as tall, typically growing only six to eight feet, making it ideal for the home-grower. Also making it ideal for the home-grower: It is great in the stress-relief, zoned-out, couch-locked kind of high that employed stoners enjoy to unwind at night. Also helpful in the treatment of insomnia.

See also **sativa**

Inhaling, the act of pulling air from the outside world into the lungs so oxygen can then enter the bloodstream and permeate the body. In a happy coincidence, this same process also allows THC to permeate the body if

one chooses to inhale marijuana smoke instead of air. The human body is not technically designed to inhale much other than normal air, so it might attempt to reject the smoke through uncontrollable spasms called "coughing." Some lucky humans have evolved beyond this unfortunate shortcoming to a point where their body actually prefers weed smoke to ordinary air.

© istockphoto / fpm

See also **controlled breathing; exhaling**

Intellectual Stoner, a variety of marijuana enthusiast who, upon smoking the leafy green substance, proceeds to spark up literary discussions, spirited political and philosophical debates, and any manner of intelligent discourse with unsuspecting individuals in the immediate vicinity. Sometimes their rants and tirades are well-researched and quite coherent, other times not so much. The intellectual stoner has mastered one important aspect of human interaction: If one says anything quickly and with authority, it is universally believed to be true.

See also active stoner; artistic stoner; casual stoner; social stoner; stoner; talkative stoner

Interstate 420, the designation of two never-built auxiliary highways that would have been built around Atlanta, Georgia, and Monroe, Louisiana, both of which would have allowed commuters to avoid the major cities through which I-20 passes. Neither road was ultimately built, however. The plan to build the road around Atlanta was derailed after communities in its path objected. Monroe's auxiliary highway was shelved after the state agreed to invest in a different highway. The proposals would have cost each state about ten times as much as their proposed budget, as every stoner in a 100-mile circumference would have jacked the signs and hung them in their bedrooms.

Introspection, the act of inward-focused thought performed by individuals seeking a greater understanding of the self that is often achieved by smoking large quantities of marijuana and assuming a contemplative position (e.g., lying in bed, sitting on a couch, or reclining in a field on one's back looking up at the clouds). This can range from the trivial "Why did I order a ham sandwich?" to deeper questions like "Where is my life going?" While it can be an enlightening experience, any insight gained is temporary, usually fading proportionally as the effects of the marijuana begin to wear off.

See also **antisocial stoner**

Jamaican Haze, the best of the original weed from Jamaica, an island nation in the Caribbean Sea where Americans vacation in order to "feel all right." Jamaica is just as much of a tropical paradise as it's depicted in pop culture, just with more crime and poverty. However, as the home of Bob Marley, Jamaica is socially obligated to offer visitors their choice of weed, and it does. Though marijuana is strictly outlawed in Jamaica, it's not uncommon to see vendors selling sticks of marijuana on buses or in the streets like they're churros. If that doesn't work, the guy standing on a street corner smoking a cigar of weed can probably lend a hit. And if he's too selfish, the guy next to him can. Or the guy next to him. It's pretty much everywhere.

Jay, a shortened slang term used in place of the slang term "joint," which itself is already plenty short enough as it is. Its existence can be seen as evidence that stoners are gradually evolving beyond the need for human speech and could progress (or regress if one wants to be a dick about it) to a point where they could communicate solely through grunts and gestures. This evolutionary leap is a necessary move if stoners are ever to solve the pesky problem of deciding whether to articulate the awesome thought they just had or to take their turn on the blunt.

See also joint

Joint, a slang term for a marijuana cigarette and is one of the most commonplace terms in the smoking culture. The word itself comes to the English language from the French word joindre (to join). While it is possible its use in reference to pot is related to the fact that various nefarious establishments such as opium dens were often called "joints," anyone who has ever smoked one knows full well that few things can join a group of people together as a smoking session does. Besides, the company that makes Pixy Stix already took the term "magic paper tube that gets you high and solves all of life's problems."

© istockphoto / xua

Journals, collections of pot-addled thoughts and ideas carried around by particularly emotional stoners like security blankets. Most stoners who write in them guard them like forbidden treasures and become extremely offended and upset if one asks to read them. However, these same stoners will also go out of their way to leave them out in the open in the hopes that somebody will read them, realize what a spectacular writer they are, and sign them to a multimillion-dollar book deal. Unfortunately, entries like, "Dear Diary, today I got high and heard color" are generally the extent of their literary prowess.

See also idea book

Junkie or Junky, one addicted to junk (heroin). In his 1953 semi-autobiographical novel *Junky*, William S. Burroughs details his experiences as a heroin user and small-time pusher in his Greenwich Village neighborhood and posits that, like marijuana, junk is not a means to a richer life, but it is itself a way of life. This is similar to marijuana. However, the junky's way of life involves prostitution, sodomy, oral sex, or any other way of debasing oneself to get heroin, instead of sitting on a couch, watching *Jeopardy* and seeing how many Twinkies one can stuff into one's mouth at one time.

Kk

K2, a synthetic compound that simulates the high of marijuana but whose side effects also include hallucinations as well as nausea and vomiting. K2 is known as "fake weed" because of its similarities to the narcotic and because it's actually legal to obtain and smoke. It was created in a lab in the 1990s by a chemist who studies cannabinoid receptors, and it is used as a plant-growth stimulant. While K2 is apparently ten times as potent as THC in marijuana and can get users very high while smoking only a small amount, its wider array of side effects make it a slightly less reliable drug. Smokers of K2 are prone to have "bad trips" more than pot smokers. Best to stick with things that grow in the ground.

Kb, a term used to describe any high-grade weed, usually some with visible THC crystals, but more commonly specific to seedless strains of incredibly potent pot. Kb is short for "kine bud," which is often misspoken as "kind bud," a pet peeve of the pretentious stoner. In fact the term "kine" derives from the Hawaiian word for "excellent" and was likely misinterpreted once the term hit the continental forty-eight. None of which matters once the stuff is smoked.

See also kind bud

Kerouac, Jack, an iconoclastic American novelist whose prose, along with Allen Ginsberg and William S. Burroughs, is primarily associated with the Beat movement. Kerouac's magnum opus is the Great American Novel *On the Road*, but he also wrote *The Dharma Bums, Mexico City Blues, The Subterraneans,* and *Visions of Cody.* The subject matter of these books often dealt with youth, travel, drugs, drinking, women, jazz clubs, transience, boxcars, and bummery. The stories are based on Kerouac's travels, and the author dabbled in illegal drugs as a youth. Still, his first love was the drink, and he died at age forty-seven from cirrhosis of the liver, cementing his legacy in American literary history. Nevertheless, every pot-smoking high-schooler, upon reading *On the Road*, dreams of living Kerouac's life. Some even bundle their clothes into a hamper, affix it to the end of a stick, and hop on the next train that stops in their town. They usually make it about six miles.

Kicked, a state of being for a bowl or bong wherein the pot that has been loaded into the head has been smoked to completion, leaving naught but ash and disappointment in its wake. Similar to the effect that occurs when one sees a sign reading "wet paint" and touches the bench just to be sure, one smoker will never take the word of another when the declaration has been made that the bowl is kicked. Once confirmation has been made that the bowl or bong is in fact kicked, a smoker needs merely to refill the piece of paraphernalia to return it to its preferred state of being.

Kief, a fine, powdery substance which is the closest thing nature has to pure THC. Consisting primarily of loose trichomes harvested from dried cannabis buds, kief is the basis for hash but can also be smoked directly or sprinkled on top of lower-quality bud as a high enhancer. Sort of like squirting chocolate syrup on boring vanilla ice cream. But way more illegal.

See also **trichomes**

Kind Bud, marijuana that is especially nice, generous, and good-natured. One of course could also be mispronouncing a specific grade of marijuana called "kine" bud, but one should know better than that by now.

See also **Kb**

Kine bud

See also kind bud; Kb.

Kush, a term often misused in reference to any variety of marijuana that is of particularly high quality. The term actually refers to a potent strain of marijuana that gets its name from the Hindu Kush mountain range located near countries in which it is grown, like India and Afghanistan. The real stuff carries a THC content of around 20 percent, more than double that of the average weed seized annually in the United States. When smoking genuine kush, it is best to do so in moderation and savor the experience. There is no telling when or if one will have the opportunity again.

See Afghan Kush

Ll

L, the twelfth letter of the alphabet and also a slang term used to describe a blunt or marijuana cigarette. Some use the term indiscriminately, but the proper usage is in reference to a specific kind of joint rolled with two perpendicular rolling papers. The resulting product is longer than a traditional joint and has a tapered shape instead of the ubiquitous uniform cylinder. Some benefits to rolling Ls include a longer burn time, more room to fit extra pot, a feeling of accomplishment, and a dramatic increase in respect among one's smoking circle.

See also joint

Laced, describes pot that has been cut with an unwanted "enhancer" such as insecticide, embalming fluid, or hard drugs like cocaine, heroin, or PCP. Some nefarious dealers will lace their subpar product in an attempt to mask the fact that it would never be able to get anybody stoned on its own. Smoking laced pot can lead to headaches, upset stomach, disorientation, and an intense desire to start paying more money for higher-quality weed.

See also dusting

Laughter, a spontaneous reaction to witnessing, hearing, or thinking something funny that is characterized by an audible response as well as physical signs like knee-slapping, tearing up, and falling on the floor. Laughter is a common side effect associated with smoking marijuana, although it is far more welcomed than some of the less desirable ones like cotton mouth and bloodshot eyes. Because of their penchant for laughter, many stoners have a skewed sense of what is and what is not funny. This is why it is important to avoid watching any of the following when sober: *Family Guy*, *Half Baked*, *Pineapple Express*, and any film starring Jack Black.

Lava Lamp, a novelty lighting device that is cool to get as an eleven-year-old. Some college dorms are decorated with lava lamps, and it's a safe bet there's also marijuana in that person's room. The various blobs of what one can only assume is molten lava rise and fall at a steady pace and are usually lighted by a colored lightbulb. Certain lamps have different settings, allowing for faster and smaller pebbles, stringy strands, or giant lava balls. Lava lamps can be stared at for hours by the marijuana-inebriated, during which time the stoner will develop emotional attachments to each bulbous glob as it passes slowly in and out of existence.

Lawnmower Bag, a large canvas container attached to a lawnmower that serves as a receptacle for grass clippings as well as an obscure hiding place for marijuana. If any suspicious police officers come snooping around in search of pot, the smell of freshly trimmed grass will mask the odor of the pot. If they should go so far as to search inside the bag, attempting to actually find the stash of weed would be like looking for a needle in a stack of needles.

Lazy Stoner, the most common breed of stoner, found in college dorm rooms, studio apartments, and the basements of millions of parents around the world. The lazy stoner lacks the motivation to do anything more strenuous than getting off the couch to load another season of *Lost* into the DVD player or stumbling into the kitchen to microwave a plate of nachos. They are a paradoxical breed, in that they often have very ambitious plans for things they will accomplish in the future, but they almost never put any of them into practice. When they run out of weed, however, they are considered to be one of the fastest beings on planet Earth, second only to a middle school pothead running away from mall security.

See also **antisocial stoner; handy stoner; hungry stoner; quiet stoner; social stoner; stoner**

Leaf, the universal symbol for marijuana that can be found adorning the hats, backpacks, T-shirts, water bottles, pants, and skin of the enlightened. Regardless of one's age, country of origin, or religious beliefs, the pot leaf is a universal symbol of 420 friendliness. Unless of course it is encased in a red circle with a slash through it. Then it's the universal symbol of assholeness.

Leech, a negative slang term used to describe a person who never has any marijuana of his or her own but is always looking to smoke someone else's stash. They are often the first ones in a group to suggest a smoking session and are frequently guilty of bogarting. Similar to the animal that shares their name, pot leeches are parasitic organisms that should be avoided at all costs.

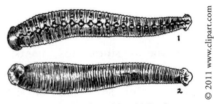

FIG. 119.—Blood-sucker, *Macrobdella decora:* 1, dorsal; 2, ventral.

See also **bogart**

Lifted, another way to describe the feeling of euphoria associated with marijuana use that is more commonly referred to as being "high." Similar to the more popular term, lifted implies general upness which is in direct contrast to the downness associated with not smoking pot.

The term first came into the public consciousness after it was used by the rapper Sir Smoke-a-Lot in the stoner film *Half Baked*. It pretty much left the stoner lexicon immediately after.

Light of Jah, a strain of marijuana known for its euphoric, sativa-like high and its tendency to grow in the shape of a Christmas tree. Stoners who take a toke of the Light of Jah after smoking only decent weed for a while may notice the high lasting longer than normal. That's because it's a stronger strain than most. Light of Jah is a favorite among the wake 'n' bake, employed, working-age pot smokers because it keeps a user functional while high, and there is minimal poststoned haze.

Light Up, a slang term used to describe the process of getting high. The phrase comes from the act of igniting the marijuana combined with the fact that getting high is synonymous with being "up." Despite the term's practicality, it is not especially welcome in the pot-smoking community. Stoners prefer terms that make no logical sense with what they mean, such as ill, bogart, and shibby.

Lighter Gnomes, small creatures who have an inexplicable affinity for unattended lighters. They frequently hide out underneath furniture, behind appliances, and on bookshelves, disguised as troll dolls. Lighter gnomes are sadistic creatures, and their single greatest pleasure is to spy on stoners, wait until they have finished packing a bowl or rolling a joint, and then strike with lightning speed to steal the lighter for their own sinister purposes. While they will occasionally steal expensive lighters, the gnomes actually prefer cheaper disposable models, perhaps counting on the fact that the owner would sooner purchase a new one than spend much time searching for the stolen item.

Lit, a slang term used to describe someone who is fairly to moderately stoned. They are most certainly high, but they are not quite baked and are definitely not yet wasted. Coincidentally, it is also the name of a quasi-popular '90s rock band that may or may not be aware of the double meaning.

Mm

Mall, The, an acreswide structure populated by Gap, Hot Topic, American Eagle, Hallmark, Foot Locker, Lady Foot Locker, Sunglass Hut, CVS, Borders, and other consumer goods stores. The mall is a destination location for stoners, who can be overwhelmed by not only the choice of stores but also the endless stream of shoppers who can't ignore the giant sales signs outside each clothing shop. Stoners are usually too indecisive to buy anything and usually end up sitting on the massage chair at Brookstone until the manager kicks them out. Stoners then meander to the food court, where they indulge in a meal of stoner delicacies: French fries, pizza, soda, Orange Julius, and sugar packets.

Manners, rules of etiquette that are associated with decency, politeness, and propriety. Simple manners include things like not eating with one's mouth open, covering one's mouth when burping, and farting as quietly as possible. However, manners are of no issue to an inebriated stoner, who can turn from the most honorable and deserving gentleman or gentlewoman into a boorish, disrespectful, brute (especially as described by English noblewomen). This can include picking their noses, scratching themselves inappropriately, wolfing down whatever edible crumbs are within sight, and generally disgusting all nonstoners in eyeshot. After all, who doesn't know that the salad fork should be held between the forefinger and thumb at a thirty-five-degree angle while piercing only three leaves of lettuce at a time and taking bites only every ten seconds or longer? Disgusting.

Marijuana, the common name for a humble little plant that has found uses in everything from religious ceremonies and medicine to orgies and music festivals. And once all four at the same time. Cannabis, as it is known in the scientific community, has been used by humans for millennia and was particularly popular among ancient Hindus who smoked it to attain spiritual enlightenment. For thousands of years it was a sacred herb that carried no negative connotations, and then all of a sudden it became a substance that was banned in the majority of the world. While historians disagree on what caused the shift in public

Male (1) and Female (2) Plants of Hemp (*Cannabis sativa*). — *a*, male flower; *b*, female flower; *c*, embryo.

opinion, it is generally believed to have had something to do with an egg and a frying pan.

See also every entry in this book

Mary Jane, a common name for human females, curiously peaking around May 15, 1970 (nine months after Woodstock). In Spanish-speaking cultures, the name is written as maria juana, which might explain why it has become synonymous with pot. If one chooses to name his or her daughter Mary Jane, one immediately waives all rights to complain when she expresses an unwavering devotion to The Grateful Dead, an insatiable appetite for Funyuns, and an inexplicable fascination with hollow household objects that don't burn easily.

Maui Wowie, a potent, sticky, bright green marijuana born in the tropical paradise that is Hawaii. Coveted by stoners the world over, the weed is regrettably found in a state consisting of a series of islands, thus making it difficult for those without flippers or wings to obtain the genuine article without purchasing an expensive plane ticket or paying a premium for an imported stash. One could try to replicate the tropical experience by lighting a few tiki torches, rolling a joint of the best local pot, and toking up to a recording of ukulele music while eating a pineapple. However, this is a surefire recipe for disappointment.

Medicinal Marijuana, a term used to describe the use of cannabis as a legitimate treatment for any range of ailments such as glaucoma, depression, nausea, and multiple sclerosis. The drug's hunger-inducing properties have also been useful for patients recovering from chemotherapy. None of the diseases, ailments, or symptoms currently treated with medicinal marijuana are particularly desirable, although the fringe benefit of legally smoking pot does take some of the edge off the ailment. As of 2010, just fourteen states have legalized the use of marijuana for medical purposes. However, that has not stopped a nation of stoners from self-medicating to cure a host of unrecognized medical conditions like head-hurts, stomach-owies, lazy legs, poor self-image, and several million raging cases of "boring Friday night in the suburbs."

Medical Marijuana Plotlines, storylines used in "edgy" sitcoms describing situations when one of the main characters begins using the drug, typically as a result of a phony illness, a pharmacy mistake, or deliberate effort. Every medical marijuana episode has the same moment: the first time the patient uses the drug and walks cooly down the sidewalk as bass guitar plays in the background. Medical marijuana plotlines are a clear sign that a sitcom is out of ideas, or, if in the third season or earlier, completely unoriginal.

Mersh, weed of subpar quality that often contains an excess of stems, seeds, and shake. While it may not be premium bud, it will certainly get the smoker high when times are tough and no superior pot can be acquired. When smoking mersh, one should keep a bottle of water handy to double as both a lubricant to counteract the effects of the harsh smoke as well as a receptacle for the unfinished joint when one gives up and goes back out to buy some decent weed.

Method, a slang term for weed that is pretty much confined to Staten Island. Luckily, much like the individuals who inhabit that area of New York, the term almost never leaves the borders of Staten Island.

Midnight Toker, an individual who indulges in a hit or two of marijuana just before bed. The term was popularized by the Steve Miller Band in their song "The Joker," in which the singer admits to being, among other things, a sinner, a lover, a smoker, a grinner, and a midnight toker. While some frown upon this practice, it is widely acceptable among the pot-smoking community as the second-best method for falling asleep. The first being to turn on old episodes of *The Joy of Painting* until Bob Ross slowly lulls one into a happy coma.

Mids, a level in the arbitrary grading of marijuana used to describe pot that isn't really great but also isn't really all that bad either. As its name implies, it is somewhere in the middle. While it isn't going to help one attain complete spiritual oneness, it is perfectly acceptable weed to smoke if one doesn't want to break the bank in the name of getting stoned.

See also chronic; headie; kind bud; kush

Milky, how one might describe a particularly large quantity of smoke accumulated in the chamber of a bong or bubbler. With a fresh bowl, long pull, and experienced bong ripper in control, the smoke can become almost completely opaque and milky in appearance. If a newbie has drawn a particularly milky cloud, a pro should probably be called in to finish off the hit, similar to calling in a pinch hitter in baseball. One doesn't want a rookie at the plate when the bases are loaded in the bottom of the ninth, metaphorically speaking.

Motivation, an internal driving force that can be severely altered by smoking pot. In sober humans, this force compels them to do everything from getting out of bed in the morning to balancing their checkbook. While motivation is not completely eliminated after smoking pot, it certainly switches gears. Instead of wanting to clean the house, a stoner might feel an intense desire to build a miniature house out of the stack of coasters on the coffee table, or watch every episode of *Arrested Development* (including the extended pilot). While these pursuits may not be as "productive" as some others, they are infinitely more gratifying.

© istockphoto / mevans

See also **lazy stoner**

Munchies, a slang term used to describe both the feeling of insatiable hunger experienced after smoking marijuana as well as the myriad snack foods smokers ingest in futile attempts to satisfy said hunger. The most satisfying foods include but are not limited to potato chips, nachos, Funyuns, cookie dough, Easy Mac, pizza, French fries, mozzarella sticks, Cheetos, White Castle Sliders, pickles, popcorn, and toast cream.

See also **appendix**

Nn

Narc, a member of the human race who has sold his or her soul to the devil in the interest of self-preservation. Usually in exchange for political amnesty, a narc agrees to cooperate with one of several government agencies and provide them with information about friends and acquaintances who engage in the buying or selling of drugs like marijuana. They are one of the lowest forms of life on the planet, ranking somewhere between tapeworms and the virus that causes AIDS.

New Caprica Leaf, aka New Caprica loco weed, a plant indigenous to the planet New Caprica whose effects appear to be similar to pot. Both Admiral Adama and President Roslin smoke the plant during a ceremony in season three, episode nine of *Battlestar Galactica* and later attempt to hide it from by-the-book officer Felix Gaeta. Roslin and Adama again smoke the leaf in the last stages of her cancer when discussing Galactica's future. New Caprica leaf serves as an escape and thought-enhancer and helps the last of the human race deal with their potential extinction. And if the reader does not watch *Battlestar Galactica*, this entry was a waste of thirty seconds.

New York Diesel, a strain of marijuana that carries the namesake of the Big Apple itself. New York Diesel mysteriously has a grape taste and smell. The high can be described as "exotic," meaning it's very heady and wavy. Seeing all the trichomes on the bud will make users want to lick the bud like a lollipop. New York Diesel is also unique in that it has starred alongside its half-brother Vin Diesel in *The Chronicles of Riddick* and the straight-to-DVD animated movie *Chronicles of Riddick: Dark Fury*, and was widely considered to have been a more believable and better actor.

Nickel Bag, a minuscule amount of marijuana which can be purchased for $5. Many years ago, this was actually a decent amount of pot. However, with the rise of inflation it currently amounts to approximately a single bowl's worth. If one is lucky. If this trend continues, a nickel bag could amount to naught but a single trichome stuck to a piece of paper. Of course, by the time this happens humans will have already been enslaved by superintelligent robots, so overpaying for pot will be the least of one's concerns.

See also **dime bag; eighth**

Nightcap, named after a warm piece of headgear that one might wear to bed before the advent of central heating, this term now refers to a small sampling of marijuana one indulges in just before retiring for the evening. As it can be difficult to smoke pot in one's sleep, this ritual is essential for anyone attempting to maintain a steady high before it's time for the morning wake 'n' bake. Sort of like a bear storing up fat for winter hibernation, but with less salmon and more smoke.

See also **wake 'n' bake**

Northern Lights, a strain of marijuana popular among home grow-ers thanks to its rapid growing cycle (about seven weeks from seed to flower) and moderately high potency. It is also rather hardy and dif-ficult to kill, a desirable trait from the perspective of a novice grower. The strain shares its name with the aurora borealis, a celestial phenom-enon in which waves of greenish light hover in the sky, occurring more frequently as one nears the North Pole. While it has never been docu-mented, there are rumors that smoking Northern Lights while observ-ing the northern lights will create a rift in the space-time continuum resulting in the end of the universe as it is known today. Please don't attempt this—just in case.

Nugs, dried buds from the female flowering cannabis sativa plant. They come in varying shapes and sizes ranging from small round peas to large conical pieces about the size of the palm. In order to be properly smoked, nugs must be delicately broken down into tiny pieces small enough to fit into the bowl of a pipe or bong. If rolling a joint, it is advisable to break the nugs up even more finely with the assistance of a grinder. Their bite-sized appearance may entice the owner to begin popping them into the mouth like bonbons. However, this temptation should be resisted if possible.

Oo

OK, a simplification of the English word okay which is generally used to say that the status of a particular person, object, or task has been deemed acceptable. The word's full potential can be realized only after one has ingested a fairly large amount of marijuana. Once in the proper state of mind, one should notice that, when written out, the word OK looks exactly like a tiny sideways person. The implications of this discovery will appear groundbreaking at first, but that feeling should diminish exponentially over time.

See also **highdea**

One Egg and a Frying Pan, according to a 1987 PSA sponsored by the Partnership for a Drug Free America, this equates to one's brain on drugs. Most stoners just see breakfast.

© istockphoto / bluestocking

One-Hitter, a small pipe that is usually just large enough to accommodate a single decent hit of marijuana. Popular among teenagers and concert-goers, one-hitters are a handy piece of paraphernalia when privacy is difficult to come by, as they often resemble ordinary cigarettes and don't draw much attention to the smoker. Their small size usually limits them to individual use; however, observational evidence has shown that desperate groups of stoners will smoke out of just about anything.

See also apple pipe; can bong; foil pipe; highlighter pipe

One-Hitter-Quitter, marijuana so potent that even the most hardened potheads are stoned off their asses after but a single puff. When one encounters bud of this quality, it is unwise to tempt fate and attempt a second hit. If one is under the impression that it is possible to keep smoking and get so high that it comes around full circle and one sobers up, then give it a try. It most certainly won't work, but it will be funny for everyone else.

One-Toke Joke, an individual who has a very low tolerance for THC and possesses the unique ability to get completely ripped off of a single hit of marijuana. While the name implies a negative connotation, frugal smokers often envy this supernatural power, longing to return to a time when they themselves could pack a single bowl of pot that would get them high for eight nights straight, like a magical marijuana menorah.

Oregano, a common herb used for culinary applications like seasoning soups, sauces, and meat. In its fresh state, it bears little resemblance to marijuana. However, when dried it could be pot's distant cousin, twice removed. For this reason, many quick-thinking stoners will attempt to convince law enforcement that their stash of pot is merely a bag of oregano they keep on hand just in case an uncontrollable urge to make pasta should arise. This is almost never believed by anyone, but it's worth a shot for the one time out of 1,000 when the cop actually falls for it.

See also **herb**

Ounce, a unit of measure in the imperial system that equates to approximately twenty-eight grams or, to the casual smoker, a pretty decent amount of herb. In twelve of the thirteen states that have decriminalized nonmedical marijuana, being caught carrying less than this amount of pot will result

© istockphoto / sumografika

in a small fine or community service, as opposed to the several months to years in federal pound-me-in-the-butt prison one might receive if found with the same amount in less forward-thinking states.

See also eighth

Pp

Pack a Bowl, a phrase uttered by pot smokers as a call to action for any other smokers within earshot who are in possession of both a stash of marijuana as well as a bowl to smoke it out of. The person making the request is often within reach of the tools necessary to make their dream of smoking more pot a reality, but they are occasionally too lazy, high, or both to do so.

Panama Red, a famous strain of marijuana indigenous to—wait for it—Panama, which has since been picked up and exported to America to take advantage of its desirable high. Panama Red was popular in the 1960s and early 1970s and is known for its high potency, ability to cause intense, psychedelic highs, and for its red, claylike color. The strain is also the inspiration behind the Jerry Garcia and Peter Rowan song "Panama Red," and it was specifically requested by the character Chef in the Vietnam War film *Apocalypse Now*. Panama Red is also the nickname given to any Panamanian pothead who joins a smoking circle, or at least it should be, i.e., "Hey Panama Red, pass that shit this way."

Paradox, a statement or argument which draws upon acceptable premises but which leads to a contradiction or a situation which defies intuition. Some examples include: 1) This statement is false, 2) What is better than eternal bliss? Nothing. But a slice of bread is better than nothing. So a slice of bread is better than eternal bliss, and 3) One's mission is not to accept this mission. Paradoxes are fun little mind teasers, except when stoners begin thinking about them too much, at which point they become the ultimate answer to what life is about. If someone is ever concerned his or her friend might be a robot or an alien, get the person high and recite a paradox. Either the alleged person's circuitry will overheat or the human form will melt, revealing a terrifying and confused creature from outer space within. If it's a real human being, the person will just sit there in stunned, blank silence.

Paranoia, a feeling that arises when one has consumed either too much bad pot or not enough good pot. Subjects will experience a sudden sense that the world is out to get them and may begin to suspect friends and family of conspiring against them. These feelings are perfectly normal and it is important not to let them interfere with the experience of being high. For example, one should not dwell on Gary, the new kid in the smoking circle who definitely looks like a narc and is totally memorizing everyone's face so he can provide accurate descriptions to the DEA officer who is absolutely waiting outside in his car right now.

See also **paranoid stoner**

Paranoid Stoner, an irritating variety of stoner who spends the majority of his or her time worrying out loud about the possibility of getting caught smoking pot. Every car with a roof rack that passes by is instantly assumed to be a cop. Each gust of wind is his or her parents coming to bust the session. While some level of paranoia can be a good thing, it is best to leave this type of stoner at home hiding in the closet where it's safe.

See also antisocial stoner; enhancement stoner; hungry stoner; lazy stoner; paranoia; social stoner; stoner; talkative stoner; violent stoner

Paraphernalia, a term used to describe various apparatuses used in conjunction with any number of different types of drugs. The DEA defines it as "any legitimate equipment, product, or material that is modified for making, using, or concealing illegal drugs such as cocaine, heroin, marijuana, and methamphetamine." In practical terms, this can apply to literally anything. Pick up the closest object to this book. Under the right circumstances, it could be considered paraphernalia. Especially if it is hollow.

See also piece

Parks, small areas of a town or city that, during the day, have been sectioned off for the purposes of hiking, bicycling, playing catch, swinging, and any number of other wholesome outdoor activities. At night, most parks are closed. However, because it is physically impossible to close off an area with no ceilings, doors, or walls, parks actually transform into a smoker's paradise shortly after dusk. With vast stretches of woods, bike paths, and gazebos to play within, a smoking session can take place without much fear of being spotted by law enforcement. When in a park, one should be on the lookout for park rangers, ticks, dog poop, and bears, all of which are sure to ruin one's buzz.

© istockphoto / bernotto

See also **woods, the**

Parking Lot, an area of real estate that has been designated for the temporary storage of automobiles. They are commonly found surrounding shopping malls, restaurants, office complexes, or anywhere humans are likely to drive to. Because they are often poorly lit, infrequently patrolled, and contain multiple exits, they are also prime locations for both the purchasing and smoking of marijuana. If police officers should happen to interrupt one's parking-lot smoking session, remember the age-old saying: "One need not run faster than the cop. Just faster than one's slowest friend."

Parsec, a unit of measure that is equal to approximately 3.26 light-years. Despite what some film directors would like to believe, it cannot be used to measure time. So the phrase, "You've never heard of the Millennium Falcon? She's the ship that made the Kessel Run in less than twelve parsecs," is the equivalent of saying, "I'm going to run down to the store to get some rolling papers. It should take me about two miles. But if I'm not back in thirty inches, just smoke without me."

Party Bong, a bong of exceptional height and girth that frequently contains several chambers and/or hoses, allowing for multiple users to smoke simultaneously. Party bongs can range from several feet to several stories in height and can be constructed out of any number of materials, from ornate glass to discarded containers of cheese balls. The latter variety may work just as well as more expensive models, although it is infinitely less likely to get the owner laid.

Party Foul, an act of stupidity, incompetence, or general douche baggery that negatively affects the well-being of every person in the near vicinity and transcends the level of mere buzzkill. Some examples include spilling bong water, volcanoing, eating all the munchies, losing the lighter, and vomiting anywhere other than a toilet or garbage can. Although the term implies there must be a large number of people present for a party foul to occur, this is a common misconception. When one drops a freshly packed bowl and watches it shatter into a hundred pieces, whether there were four witnesses or 400, one is still an asshole.

See also **buzzkiller**

Passing Out, the act of losing consciousness due to an excessive amount of drug ingestion, usually taking place on a couch or in a ditch. Passing out is a time-honored tradition usually resulting from the body's overwhelming desire to sleep and rid itself of the toxins that the drug user has pumped into his or her body. While usually harmless in one's own bed, passing out with friends still in one's presence is an invitation to have the passer-outer's body covered in Sharpie drawings of penises and insults, having pictures taken of such drawings on the person's body, and having said pictures posted to Facebook.

Pay phone, an archaic device that allows humans to communicate with one another for a nominal fee. Since being replaced by the cellular telephone, the pay phone has been relegated to use solely as a means for coordinating drug deals. While cell phone conversations can be traced and recorded, there is not much benefit to tracing a pay phone. Once the police arrive they would be far more likely to find a bum rifling through the coin slot than anybody trying to score some weed.

Perma-Burned, a state of being that results from an extended period of steady marijuana use. The subject will often exhibit the telltale signs of being stoned (lethargy, intense relaxation, euphoria, introspective thought, and insatiable hunger) but may not have actually smoked pot in several days, months, or even years. Those outside the smoking community often look down upon those suffering from this common affliction. However, many stoners actually strive for this state of being. It's like attaining spiritual oneness without the religious overtones and false sense of superiority.

Pickle Juice, a liquid compound found almost exclusively inside of pickle jars that is rumored to have magical properties. Many people believe that, when ingested in large quantities, it erases any evidence of recent drug use should the drinker be subjected to several forms of drug testing, both random and anticipated. Many people also believe in Santa Claus.

Piece, a generic term used to refer to any structure used for smoking marijuana that can be used multiple times. This can include bongs, bowls, chillums, pipes, hookahs, and anything that one would be proud to whip out during a session. For this reason, a piece of foil one has folded into the shape of a pipe does not qualify, regardless of how long it took the creator to produce.

Pinner, a very small, tightly wrapped marijuana cigarette which frequently contains more paper than actual weed. One generally rolls a pinner only when one is not in possession of enough pot to roll a respectable joint or pack a bowl but would still like the experience of inhaling smoke from a burning piece of paraphernalia. By itself, a pinner is not enough to get the average smoker very high, but it can make for an excellent appetizer before a main course of bong hits or blunts and also doubles as a delightful nightcap. Its existence reminds the world that it is not the size of the joint that matters, but what one does with it.

See also **vegetarian joint**

Pipe, a device used for smoking marijuana, which is often used synonymously with "bowl." In some cultures, a pipe is slightly different from a bowl in that there is no carb present to allow air to circulate when inhaling. They are prized for their portability, versatility, and inexpensive cost of ownership. While they are generally made from metal, wood, or glass, research has shown that they can also be crafted out of any number of common household objects such as cans, pens, aluminum foil, fruit, and nearly anything that isn't flammable—and even a few things that are.

Pipe Weed, a type of herb smoked by hobbits and various other races in the Middle Earth realm of J. R. R. Tolkien's *The Lord of the Rings*. There are a number of varieties available throughout the land. However, no self-respecting hobbit would smoke anything other than Longbottom Leaf. Unless of course it was just after second breakfast and somebody else was offering.

Playgrounds, small parks filled with slides, jungle gyms, seesaws, swings, and that stupid tic-tac-toe game nobody ever plays. During the day, hordes of screaming children have free rein over these playgrounds, but at night they become popular hangouts for stoners looking to toke up and relive their youth. The tube slide is an especially popular attraction for pot smokers, as it offers cover from police officers and also provides a cheap thrill to the stoner when he or she is finished smoking. One should not attempt to operate the swings while high, due to the increased risk of pumping too hard, flipping over the bar, and turning one's body inside out.

Pockets, small crevices woven into pants, shirts, hoodies, and jackets, which can be used to store small amounts of marijuana and associated paraphernalia. They can also be used to store cell phones, money, MP3 players, and hands (when not in use). They may not seem like much, but one would be wise to remember that it would be next to impossible to smoke pot without them. If one does not believe this, try turning them inside out and get ready to go smoke pot at a friend's house. Not so easy, is it?

© istockphoto / SasPartout

Poker, an essential instrument when smoking from a bong that does exactly what its name implies—it pokes things. Specifically, it pokes ash, resin, and stray pieces of dust through the bowl head and into the chamber of the bong so that it can be later flushed away the next time the owner decides to get off his or her lazy ass and clean the bong. While there are dedicated pokers specifically built for this function, a paper clip, safety pin, or any long and thin apparatus will suffice.

See also **stoke**

Pollinator, a type of multitiered grinder that contains a fine mesh screen above the bottom level which can be used to filter out all smokable plant material, leaving behind the THC-bloated trichomes. If one has a lot of time, patience, and the proper equipment, one can use these harvested trichomes to create hashish. However, if one is like most stoners, one can simply sprinkle the trichomes on top of the weed about to be smoked, thus negating the entire reason for purchasing a pollinator.

See also **grinder**

Pot, a slang term used to refer to marijuana, the popularity of which rivals that of the euphemism "weed." The word is probably a shortening of a Spanish word for marijuana, potiguaya. A few people believe it is in reference to how the drug affects the human mind and body, in that it makes the user feel like an inanimate cooking utensil. There is little to no evidence to defend this theory, but it certainly sounds plausible.

© istockphoto / rodehi

Pothead, a derogatory term directed toward people who smoke marijuana to excess. While many nonsmokers use this term as a blanket descriptor for all people who smoke weed, this is a misconception. A pothead smokes at least five times a day and has given up on all life pursuits that are not directly related to the acquisition and subsequent smoking of weed. In the late '70s, a simple test was developed to determine if someone was in fact a pothead, and it can still be used today. A small amount of pot is placed on a table next to a lighter and a crisp $100 bill in an empty room. If the subject pockets the money and leaves, the subject is a square. If the subject pockets the money first and then the pot, the subject is merely a stoner. If the subject scans the scene, uses the money to roll a joint, and lights up, he or she is most certainly a pothead. Or a very wealthy stoner.

Power Hit, a single hit of marijuana that defies the ordinary limits of the human body. When a smoker takes a power hit, he or she proceeds to exhale clouds of smoke as onlookers watch in horror as a thick gray cloud continues to billow out long after the threshold of human lung capacity has been exceeded. Witnessing this event is a cause of celebration, however, as it is believed to indicate that 420 will come early that particular year. Unless of course the stoner sees his or her shadow, in which case the group must wait until April 20 to celebrate.

Pregnant, a slang term used to refer to a marijuana cigarette that has an unbalanced level of pot sitting in the middle, causing the joint to bulge outward. This is terrible news for someone who will get the joint at the beginning or end of a session. This is joyous news, however, if one happens to be in the middle of the smoking circle. Be wary of someone who offers to roll a joint only under the condition that he or she can choose the smoking order.

© istockphoto / Andreas Weber

Puff, a word used to denote a single intake of marijuana; it is synonymous with the term "hit." It can also be used in reference to the general experience of smoking marijuana, similar to "toke" or "get high." It could theoretically be used as a slang term for a species of penguinlike bird called the "puffin," but there are no examples for when that might be appropriate in the context of smoking marijuana. Or life in general.

Puff, Puff, Pass, a common method of smoking marijuana wherein participants organize themselves in a static configuration, preferably a circle, and take two hits before passing the smoking apparatus of choice to the next person. In general this process has proved to be an effective method of ensuring each smoker receives an equal amount of marijuana. However, a strange phenomenon has been known to occur wherein otherwise intelligent individuals struggle with rudimentary concepts like counting to two, telling time, and differentiating between right and left.

"Puff the Magic Dragon," a song based on a poem written by Leonard Lipton and popularized by the band Peter, Paul and Mary about a little boy and his magical dragon who lives in a land called Honah Lee. Or a song based on a poem written by Leonard Lipton and popularized by the band Peter, Paul and Mary all about smoking pot and getting high. The song features a little boy named Jackie Paper (read: rolling papers) and a whimsical dragon named Puff (read: toke, drag, hit). While the song's creators insist it has abso-lutely nothing to do with Mary Jane, the urban leg-end has become so perva-sive that Ben Stiller cites it as fact in the 2000 film *Meet the Parents*. And as anyone knows, if Ben Stiller says it, then it must be true.

© istockphoto / Polkan61

See also **euphemisms**

Pull, the act of putting one's lips to the end of a smoking apparatus, be it joint, blunt, bong, bowl, hookah, or chillum, and sucking smoke into the lungs. While there are plenty of other slang terms used to describe this process, the powers that be felt one more was in order. Similar to the human pyramid, it does not need to exist. But it's nice to know it's there.

Purple Haze, a particularly potent strain of cannabis known for its violet-tinted trichomes and for providing a clean, energetic high. The debate over what came first—the weed or the Hendrix song—is a frequent argument among stoners, though it's most likely that the plant was named after the tune. Despite the musician's repeated denials, many fans believe the song's true inspiration to be a superpotent form of LSD that was served up on purple blotters at the 1967 Monterey Pop Festival, at which Hendrix performed. Absurd urban legends persist that Purple Haze is, itself, laced with a powerful hallucinogenic drug. Not so. It's just that good.

Qq

Quality, a term used to refer to the inherent level of goodness an object possesses. In some instances this can be relatively arbitrary, such as is the case with brands of baking soda. However, items like marijuana have very tangible differences that can be used to assess quality. Weight, color, moisture content, visual evidence of trichomes and crystals, fragrance, and taste can all determine the quality of a sample of weed. However, like many things, quality is relative when it comes to pot. Somebody who has smoked schwag all his or her life is easily pleased.

See also **schwag**

Quantity, a term used to refer to how much of a certain item one is currently in possession of, or, in the abstract sense, how much one would like to possess. In the landmark Supreme Court decision of Quantity v. Quality (Nashville, December Term, 1926), quantity was in fact ruled to be better than quality. In regards to marijuana, however, this amount should never exceed the maximum capacity of one's mouth and stomach, as it may be necessary to eat the pot while fleeing from law enforcement officials. While this will not be well received by the stomach, or the rest of the body for that matter, it is almost always better than jail.

Quap, a slang term used when purchasing large amounts of marijuana that refers to four ounces, or approximately one quarter of one pound. The average smoker will never purchase this much pot for personal use, so this is a term reserved primarily for dealers and groups of friends buying in bulk. Many stoners often dream of purchasing a quap and using it to roll one giant blunt. However, the $1,000 price tag generally deters all but the most dedicated smokers.

Quiet Stoner, a type of pot aficionado whose body chemistry reacts with THC in such a way that he or she becomes completely incapable of human speech immediately after ingesting pot. These stoners will often appear attentive and involved in whatever event or conversation is going on around them. However, they will make no attempt to communicate with anyone in the group. Depending on their normal demeanor, this can be either a welcome break from their loudmouthed persona or simply par for the course with their usual sheepish disposition. In either case, it's best not to draw attention to their lack of verbal interaction.

See also **antisocial stoner; artistic stoner; enhancement stoner; intellectual stoner; lazy stoner; paranoid stoner; stoner**

Rr

Rastafarian, a religious affiliation characterized by dreadlocks; Bob Marley music; Jamaican accents; red-, white-, green-, and black-striped woven caps; and excessive consumption of marijuana. The movement started in the 1930s and was born out of the Christianity that had consumed Jamaica in the nineteenth century when British Christian abolitionists joined former slaves in the struggle to end slavery. Rastas believe that they and all members of the African diaspora are exiles in Babylon and are destined to return to Zion, led by Haile Selassie I, the former emperor of Ethiopia. Not knowing this, many white American hippies often claim to be Rasta in an effort to come across as both trendy and worldly, and to legitimize their pot habits. Everyone else, however, outside of maybe their hippie friends, laughs behind their back.

Reefer, a slang term for marijuana generally employed by people who don't smoke marijuana. Such people are also prone to calling it "dope," "wacky tobacky," "puff the magic dragon," or "whatever you call that stuff that all the kids are smoking these days."

Resin, the sticky residue of burned pot that collects inside of pieces or other smoking devices. This substance is particularly harsh but can be smoked if one's connect gets burned. In dire situations, bowls and slides can be scraped and the resultant resin smoked again. Kind of the equivalent of a dog eating the same ice cream cone twice.

See also **hot knifing**

Roach, a slang term used to describe a marijuana cigarette, more specifically the small nubbin left once a joint has been smoked as far down as is possible without burning the fingertips. Without the aid of a roach clip, a roach is one of the most useless things known to modern man. With the aid of a roach clip, however, it is magically transformed into a delectable afternoon treat. Over time, many roaches can be saved up and combined into a bowl or even a new joint, beautifully illustrating the process of rebirth pervasive in many religions.

See also **joint**

Roach Clip, any nonflammable object that can be employed to hold the end of a marijuana cigarette to prevent injury to the hands and fingers of the smoker. A hemostat is the preferred instrument, although smokers without access to surgical equipment have been known to use everything from simple paper clips and forks to artificial limbs.

Robotripping, a high obtained by consuming large quantities of the chemical dextromethorphan, which is found in over-the-counter cough medications like Robitussin. Hence the name. While the name implies that one might experience a hallucinogenic trip similar to taking drugs like LSD or shrooms, hallucinations are actually fairly rare. What one will experience is reduced motor function, a feeling of being out of one's body, a near-catatonic dreamlike state, and distinct feelings of embarrassment associated with downing an entire bottle of cough syrup just to get high.

Roll, the act of creating a joint, spliff, blunt, or other rolled marijuana-consumption device. After a lengthy debate over who is the best roller, or whose dad once rolled a joint with one hand while driving eighty miles an hour down I-90, stoners eventually decide who will be rolling the joint for the session. The designated roller should be one with a proven track record of well-formed joints and not just a weekend warrior who watched *Almost Famous* the night before.

© istockphoto / KarenMassier

Technique is of the utmost importance, and experienced rollers will have a well-defined style or hallmark to their joints. The seasoned hand-roller will also consider those who use auto-rollers total wusses.

Rollers, a device that takes all of the guesswork out of rolling a joint and produces them mechanically. The device consists of two parallel bars that spin in a circular motion. Marijuana is loaded between the rollers, which are then spun to distribute the pot in an even layer. Finally, a sheet of rolling papers is inserted between the bars, which are then spun a final time to produce a perfectly packed jay. For smokers lacking the dexterity to produce a perfect joint by hand, this device allows them to smoke on their own without the need to seek out friends with more nimble fingers.

Rolling Papers, thin sheets of material usually made from hemp, wood pulp, or rice, which can be used to transform loose tobacco, marijuana, or other herbs into a neat, uniform tube just begging to be smoked. It may be illegal to purchase rolling papers for use with marijuana. However, it is also illegal to pull the little tags off of pillows, and that doesn't seem to stop too many people, either.

Running, a recreational activity one can indulge in when one has not done anything illegal recently, or a necessary response when one is smoking pot and encounters the flashing lights of a police car or an authoritative voice asking, "Hey, what's going on over there?" It is similar to walking, only much faster (hopefully) and carries a greater sense of urgency.

See also **dark alley**

Rush, a feeling of euphoria one experiences after engaging in activities like bungee jumping, sexual intercourse, or smoking marijuana. The feeling is a result of several chemicals in one's body, such as adrenaline and dopamine, being released in the interest of self-preservation or as reward for doing something the body considers to be a good idea. Clearly the body is never wrong, so this phenomenon is considered irrefutable evidence that smoking pot is, in general, a wise decision. By this logic, similar wise decisions include: jumping out of airplanes, grand theft auto, bare-knuckle boxing, and purposely engaging and subsequently fleeing from stampeding bulls.

Ss

Salad Bowl, a single bowl of pot that contains multiple strains of marijuana, usually resulting from a number of participants contributing a small portion from their own personal stashes. When the varieties mix, the end result can be either a glorious marriage of flavors and attributes from a mosaic of top-grade pot or a disastrous combination of dried-up schwag. If one's weed already sucks, combining it with equally poor-quality bud isn't going to make it suck any less.

Sativa, one of the two meta-categorizations of marijuana, along with indica. Sativa is slightly different from indica in that its leaves are longer and thinner (often the pot leaf represented in pop culture) as opposed to shorter and stubbier. And the high is more uplifting and, depending

© 2011 www.clipart.com

on circumstances, energizing. Sativa is for the daytime smoker, and many strands allow smokers to remain upbeat and productive. Sativa is also typified by its height, growing as much as twenty-five feet high, and its branches can extend up to three feet, making it largely grown as wild marijuana and not in urban areas.

See also indica

Scale, a device used to measure weight that can range from the complex digital variety to less complex mechanical versions. Scales are an invaluable tool for drug dealers who use them to ensure their product is evenly broken down from bulk amounts into smaller increments for resale. The credibility of a dealer can often be determined by the sophistication of the scale he or she employs. If it's digital, it's safe to assume he or she is on the up-and-up. If he or she employs the "hold something of comparable weight in each hand and see which feels heavier" approach, then it might be wise to buy elsewhere.

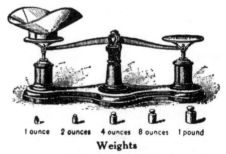

1 ounce   2 ounces   4 ounces   8 ounces   1 pound

Weights

© 2011 www.clipart.com

See also eighth; ounce

Schwag, a term used to define marijuana that is of the lowest-available quality. This grade of weed can hardly be considered pot, as it is frequently little more than a conglomeration of stems, oregano, and dried-up shake. It is not recommended that schwag be smoked unless under the most dire of circumstances, such as when one flushes his higher-grade stash down the toilet during an unfortunate bout of paranoia.

See also **stress**

Score, the physical act of obtaining weed from a dealer, friend, relative, stranger, homeless person, or hyperintelligent gorilla capable of communicating through gestures. The term is so named because the feeling of transforming from a person who is in need of pot to a person possessing one's own marijuana is akin to earning a point in every game played by modern humans while simultaneously having sex with multiple partners.

Screen, a small, thin piece of rigid mesh material (usually metal) that is placed inside of a bowl, pipe, or other smoking device to prevent unwanted ash particles from entering the mouth and lungs of the user. Many types of paraphernalia do not come with screens. However, they can be purchased at any hardware store for several cents and cut down to the preferred size. Despite their inexpensive cost and ready availability, it usually requires no fewer than seven unintentional inges-tions of hot ash before the average stoner builds up the motivation necessary to install one.

Sculpture, the preferred deflection used to explain the existence of a large glass bong, bubbler, or pipe on the dress-ers of countless stoners around the world. When asked why the sculpture conspicu-ously smells like pot, the only acceptable response is, "How do you know what pot smells like?" This will usually result in the nosy person mumbling an apology and shuffling out of the room.

© istockphoto / josh-r

Secondhand Smoke, a by-product of the process of igniting any smokable product (tobacco, marijuana, hashish, etc.) and inhaling the resulting dark cloud. After a period of time, the smoke must be exhaled from the lungs and into the air. As a result, individuals in the surround-ing area can be exposed to the THC-laden smoke and get high through no direct effort of their own. This passive form of smoking is ideal for frugal stoners who would like to get high but prefer not actually to pay for it.

Seeds, tiny, hard, circular objects contained within the innards of a plant or fruit. Seed presence in a baggie means the weed purchase is slightly overpriced, as seeds weigh more than the plant and are also unsmokable. Smoking seeds would result in nausea, bad headache high, and painful moaning. However, seeds can be useful for the indus-trious stoner, as they can be planted to create new and free marijuana. Germinating and growing weed from seeds can be as simple as pur-chasing a pot, dirt, and plant food. However, when inebriated, ston-ers will typically try to bypass this process and just plant the seeds in dirt and "see if it works." Usually, they just end up with a frown and much time wasted.

© istockphoto / BenDower

Sensi, short for "sensimilla," a colloquial Anglicization of the Spanish term "sin semilla," meaning "no seeds," or marijuana produced from an unfertilized female cannabis plant. The upside of sensi is that, because the plant's THC-packed buds never mature into seeds, the resulting harvest is chock-full of baked-inducing goodness. The downside is that, due to the lack of seeds, it's impossible to breed sensi-producing plants. This harsh botanical reality makes sensi a pricier toke than other seedier brands, but that's all right. Seedless is always better. Seedless grapes. Seedless watermelons. One can only imagine how good ranch-flavored sunflower seeds would taste if they were just flavor-packed bundles of unmitigated ranch.

Session, a discrete instance of one or more persons inhaling marijuana with the intent of achieving a high. Sessions have been known to spontaneously occur in bathrooms, cars, the woods, dorm rooms, and any place with a high concentration of boredom and video games.

Shake, a dried-up conglomeration of marijuana particles left at the bottom of a bag of weed. Little preparation needs to be done to the actual marijuana before smoking shake, as it does not need to be removed from a stem and/or ground. Still, one most take several measures to prepare the body. It is important to have no fewer than four Marlboro Reds immediately prior, as the harsh cigarette smoke acts as a buffer for what will certainly be equally harsh shake smoke. Stretching is not necessary, although it is advisable in case one needs to run to grab a glass of water in the event of a coughing fit. Lastly, one should eliminate any expectations of enjoying this particular smoking experience and focus instead on not waiting so long before buying more pot in the future.

Shampoo Bottles, containers of varying shapes and sizes used to house a hair-cleansing product known as "shampoo." Because shampoo has a reputation for covering up unpleasant odors, the bottles are often used for the storing and transporting of marijuana. In theory, if one were to nestle a small amount of pot in with the shampoo, unknowing humans would be fooled into believing one intends to use it to stay clean and fresh rather than as a means of getting baked. It is best not to employ this trick in the presence of drug-sniffing dogs, as they are far more intelligent than the average human and will see right through the ruse.

Shibby, a term popularized in the stoner film *Dude, Where's My Car?* whose mystery is exceeded only by its power. The word is synonymous with any of the following words or phrases: cool, stoned, sweet, happy, mellow, drunk, awesome, message, attractive, smart, enlightened, really stoned, confused, hungry, and literally anything else the user wants it to imply. Shibby will undoubtedly be considered the most versatile word in the English language if the editors at Merriam-Webster ever get high enough to allow it to slip in.

© istockphoto / dimol

Shiva, the Hindu god of destruction and reproduction, one of the five primary forms of God in the Hindu faith, and a deity who is often depicted with a third eye, with which he burned Desire to ashes. Marijuana is associated with worshiping Shiva, who is popularly believed to like the plant and is often depicted in images with it. During the Shivaratri festival (or "Great night of Shiva"), followers offer the god bhang, a liquid form of the drug that varies in strength based on how much pot is used. Bhang is not only offered to Shiva but also consumed by the god's followers, and smoked cannabis is seen as a gift to Shiva to aid in sadhana, or "a means to accomplishing something." Pot smokers would be wise to be knowledgeable about such matters, as the excuse can be used to get out of jams with teachers, parents, police officers, or judges.

Shoe Tossing, the mysterious practice of tying shoes together by the laces and flinging them over power lines and telephone wires. The practice takes place in both rural and urban areas, and while not definitively known, several theories exist to explain the occurrences. Among the most popular is that shoes hanging from telephone lines mark areas where drugs are sold, and that if a buyer stands under one of them long enough, a dealer will come to hook the person up. Unfortunately, it is impossible to hang out underneath a pair of hanging shoes without everyone in the immediate vicinity knowing precisely what one is doing there.

Shoes, articles of clothing used to protect the feet from injury that double as a low-tech method for hiding and transporting marijuana. Because of the undesirable odor of the human foot, some law enforcement agents are reluctant to check a suspect's shoes when searching for contraband. While this method carries with it the unfortunate side effect of making one's pot smell like feet, it's a small price to pay for not going to jail.

Shotgun, a complex maneuver wherein one smoker inserts a lit joint or blunt into his or her mouth, burning end first, while another positions his or her face directly in front of the other end. The first participant then blows out, unleashing a cloud of concentrated smoke into the mouth of the other. There have been no reported fatalities as a result of this practice. However, the number of burnt tongues and bruised egos resulting from failed attempts is too high to calculate.

See also **French inhale**

Shrooms, a slang term used to refer to psilocybin mushrooms, a breed of fungi that, when ingested, stimulate a psychedelic experience known colloquially as a "trip." Because they occur naturally in the wild, shrooms are embraced by stoners adhering to the "if it grows from the ground, it's probably okay" philosophy. When taking shrooms, it is a good idea to have some marijuana handy to smoke as one comes down from the trip. It eases the transition from euphoric utopia to disappointing reality.

SINO, a stoner in name only. SINOs are people who would ordinarily be called a stoner based on how often they get high but who don't possess the adequate skills, experiences, or interests of the larger stoner zeitgeist and thus don't represent stoner culture at large. This would include people who haven't seen *Half Baked*, people who wear a suit or dress to work, people with good personal hygiene, married people over thirty-five, professional sprinters, people who abstain from alcohol, Jehovah's Witnesses, etc. This is in contrast to the SIEW, a stoner in every way, which would include people who listen to Hendrix, people who own the two-disc version of *Being John Malkovich*, people who shop at Old Navy, professional cross-country runners, and people who write books called *The Danktionary*.

Skins, a slang term for rolling papers popular among time-strapped stoners who can't be bothered with multiple syllables. The term derives from the fact that if a joint were a person, the papers would be its skin. Extrapolating this analogy, one can deduce that the cherry would be its mouth, the unlit end would be its anus, the pot would be its internal organs, and the person smoking it would be God.

Skunk, a slang term used to describe highly potent and odoriferous weed. The term derives from a small furry mammal of the family mephitidae that is generally black with one or more white strips running down the length of its back. The animal has the ability to secrete a highly offensive smell from anal scent glands located near the base of the tail. While encountering the mammal is often an undesirable experience, encountering skunky weed is almost always a cause for celebration. Usually in the form of smoking it.

Slide, an element of a bong that acts similarly to a carb, allowing air to flow into the chamber and push the smoke into the user's lungs when removed from the bong. Unlike with a carb, the user does not need to actively cover a hole to work the apparatus, but instead simply leaves the slide in place when pulling the hit and removes it when it is time to inhale the delicious smoke. In most cases the slide serves double duty as the receptacle into which the marijuana is packed before being smoked. Smokers attempting to make the transition from carb to slide should observe others first, as there are few things more embarrassing than waiting for one's turn to smoke, inconspicuously inspecting the bong for a hole, scratching one's head, and sheepishly asking, "So now what?"

Slinging, the act of attempting to move drugs either on the street corner, in a park, under a lamp-post, or in any other type of drive-through-style ordering situation. The term derives from the way drugs were dealt in the old days, when cars would flash their lights at the dealer and slowly pass them

© istockphoto / Sirimo

by on the street. The dealer would then use a slingshot to try to make the baggie fly through the car's window. If the dealer missed, the buyer got the baggie free. If he made it, the driver also got the baggie free since they were in a car and the dealer was on foot. As such, old-school slinging as a means of dealing drugs quickly grew out of favor and has been replaced by the more traditional means of someone approaching a shady character on the street and simply asking, "Yo, you got shit?"

Slobber, an excessive accumulation of human saliva, which is an unfortunate side effect of sharing a joint or blunt with multiple parties. When some people take a hit, they mistake the joint or blunt for an attractive member of their preferred sex and engage in deep, passionate French kissing with it. This is a common mistake and, like most things in life, can easily be remedied with incessant name-calling.

Smoke, a by-product of combustion that results when burning any form of matter. It is usually a thin gray or black wispy substance that floats in the air and dissipates over time. Smoke can be either undesirable or desirable, depending on the circumstances. When it is evidence that one's house is about to burn to the ground, it is especially unwelcome. When it is evidence that one's friends are getting high and one should join in, it is most welcome.

Smoking, the preferred method for ingesting marijuana among the majority of stoners. One generally inserts the marijuana into a bong, bowl, joint, blunt, or other receptacle, ignites it with a lighter or matches, inhales the resulting THC-laden by-product known as smoke into the lungs, and exhales. When done correctly, several minutes later the subject will be stoned. When done incorrectly, several minutes later the subject will be confused and embarrassed—but certainly not stoned.

© istockphoto / graphixel

Smoke-In, a large gathering of pot smokers in numbers too great for authorities to arrest everyone. A form of peaceful protest, the first of which was held in Washington, D.C., on July 4, 1970, when 25,000 stoners participated. It continues to this day.

Snootchie Bootchies, a catchphrase uttered by Jason Mewes frequently when portraying his trademark character, Jay, in one of Kevin Smith's many stoner films. It's meaning is pretty open to interpretation and serves as a deflection to draw attention away from an exceptionally crass and uncalled-for remark. For example one might say, "Last night I stole all your pot, fucked your sister, and then set your house on fire. Snootchie bootchies!" The person hearing this news would potentially be so confused by what was meant by "snootchie bootchies" that he or she would completely ignore the far more offensive aspects of the statement.

Snow Bong, an ordinary bong that has been enhanced with the addition of crisp, clean, wintry snow. Preferably white and definitely not yellow. The user packs the chamber completely full of snow instead of water and then proceeds to smoke as normal. The snow will then cool the smoke as it makes its way to the user's lungs. For some stoners, this is literally the only good thing about winter.

© istockphoto / eddyfish

Snow White, a character in a fairy tale involving seven dwarfs, a magic mirror, an apple, and of course a prince, and is the namesake of a potent, white-tinted strain of marijuana that is known for its potent, mellow high. With big round leaves and fat buds, the pot is just as beautiful as the fairy-tale character. And if one kisses it, Snow White the weed also awakens and fills the user with love. Except, also like the fairy tale's postscript, that feeling lasts only about five hours before the slow descent back to reality begins.

Snuffing, an oft-overlooked form of pot etiquette wherein the smoker, after he or she has taken a hit and before passing to the next person, uses a lighter to extinguish the burning marijuana and prevent any of the precious leaf from being wasted. Some absentminded stoners will often snuff the bowl but subsequently remember an important and elaborate story that must be shared with the group immediately and forget the necessary proceeding step of passing it along in the circle. Depending on how long the session has been in progress, this can go unnoticed by the rest of the circle for several minutes or several hours.

Social Stoner, a person who smokes very infrequently and exclusively during social situations like parties and, well, pretty much just at parties. They are extremely prone to smoking gaffes like volcanoing, babysitting, and slobbering simply because they do not smoke frequently enough to have learned how to avoid these embarrassing faux pas. This is often the first stage of a stoner's life cycle, in which the subject is capable of metamorphosing into any number of other stoner personas. For this reason one should avoid getting them wet or feeding them after midnight, as there's no telling what might happen.

See also **active stoner; antisocial stoner; casual stoner; enhancement stoner; intellectual stoner; paranoid stoner; stoner**

Sock Drawer, a widely utilized and relatively obvious location for hiding any number of private items ranging from condoms and dildos to money and jewelry to marijuana and rolling papers. The assumption of the hiding place is that no self-respecting parent or police officer would resort to rifling through smelly socks when looking for contraband. This assumption is inherently flawed, as all evidence shows that most parents and police officers have little to no respect for privacy.

© istockphoto / wynnter

See also shoes

Spaced Out, a common state among absentminded pot smokers resulting in an unusually slow reaction time to external stimuli. The term gets its name from the fact that subjects will usually just sit and stare off into space for extended periods of time. They might be looking at something interesting, like a pretty picture or a funny movie. However, they are often just gazing off into the distance. There is no surefire cure for spacing out, although lighting up another joint has an uncanny ability to snap them back to attention, albeit temporarily.

Spark, a small glowing ember of matter that has the ability to ignite certain gases to create fire, and an essential element for smoking pot. It also serves as a form of pot slang used as a call to action when followed by the words "it" and "up."

Spliff, a slang term that generally refers to a long conical marijuana cigarette containing both tobacco and cannabis. One might choose to roll such a joint in order to extend the life of a dwindling stash of weed, as a clever misdirection in an elaborate bogarting scheme, or to mask the smell and taste of particularly low-grade schwag in order to avoid public humiliation. Some self-loathing stoners will roll them instead of a full joint because they are embarrassed by their smoking habit and are trying to cut back. One should never roll a spliff for this reason, as one has nothing to be ashamed of.

Spoof, an ingenious contraption common in college dorm rooms that is used to mute the smell of marijuana. The device consists of a paper towel or toilet paper roll stuffed with dryer sheets, which are occasionally sprayed with cologne, Febreze, or any other fragrance. With spoof in hand, the smoker will take a hit as normal, but when it comes time to exhale he or she will do so into one end of the tube. Unfortunately for stoners, the spoof's scent-masking abilities share one important characteristic with the fairies in J.M. Barrie's *Peter Pan*—they only exist if the user believes in them.

Square, a geometric shape that makes for a poor configuration for smoking pot in groups as it requires an even number of people to create. It is also a term used to refer to anyone who does not indulge in smoking, eating, smelling, touching, looking at, or even thinking about marijuana. Oftentimes squares look down on cannabis smokers and will say mean things about them. Sometimes, however, their prejudice is not truly their fault. They have merely been misinformed and there is still hope that they can be shown the light. But one should not hold his or her breath.

Stash, a stockpile of marijuana that is almost always hidden in a location believed by the owner to be completely obscure and undetectable, but is actually wildly obvious and cliché (e.g., inside a cigar box, velvet pouch, mattress, or hollowed-out dictionary). If one's stash is located by parents, police officers, a nosy significant other, or drug-sniffing dogs, there is only one appropriate response: "So that's where that went. Now I can finally hand it over to the proper authorities."

Stash Can, a clever apparatus used for hiding illicit items like marijuana and condoms from parents and nosy roommates. To create, one simply takes an ordinary soda can and removes the top with a can opener. After discarding the contents, one inserts a smaller glass jar with a twist-off lid and attaches said lid to the underside of the removed can top. Now, one simply places any contraband inside of the jar and seals the device with the lid/top combo. The result is a completely foolproof hiding place. Unless of course somebody tries to drink it.

Stems, the structural support system for the cannabis sativa plant that allow for the blooming of buds and flowers. While this function is admirable, once the buds have been harvested the stems are more or less useless and should be discarded before selling. If one discovers a stem in one's stash, one should alert the dealer from whom it was purchased immediately. If the dealer is unwilling to rectify the situation, there is absolutely nothing one can do about it, as there is currently no customer service center in existence that one can call to report poor drug-dealing service.

Sticky Icky, a slang term used to describe bud that is especially potent, dank, skunky, etc. High-grade marijuana that has been properly cured is slightly sticky to the touch, as opposed to schwag, which is generally dry as a bone. Industrious DIY dealers often attempt to resuscitate their dried-up low-grade pot by adding sticky substances such as honey, molasses, or sugar and passing it off as sticky weed. There is a special place in hell for these people, right alongside telemarketers and meter maids.

See also schwag

Stoke, the physical act of cleaning a bong, pipe, chillum, bubbler, bowl, or any apparatus used for the purpose of smoking marijuana. Over time, tar, resin, and bong water can cause a piece to become discolored and even obstruct the chamber, making it nearly impossible to get high efficiently. This is unacceptable and should be remedied at the earliest convenience. Depending on how thorough the owner of the dirty piece is, this can range in anything from filling the paraphernalia with water, closing both ends, and shaking it around to painstakingly rubbing the inside with pipe cleaners and lovingly applying dedicated cleaning solutions like Formula 420. Some smokers claim that, similar to the way a well-seasoned grill imparts flavor to meat, an unclean bong makes for more potent bud.

See also Formula 420

Stoned, the state of being intoxicated via marijuana consumption. "Getting stoned" is one of the most common phrases to refer to smoking weed, yet its origin remains an unsettled question to most stoners.

Some claim the term derives from an old alcoholic drink called Stone Fence. Another theory claims "being stoned" refers to the act of a stone: doing nothing. But most etymologists agree the term derives from 1930s slang for being intoxicated, as people would wobble around as if they had just been stoned by an angry mob. That tradition carries on today, just with less blood and death.

Stoner, a person or animal that frequently gets high by smoking or ingesting buds from the cannabis sativa plant. Nonsmoking members of society often use the term as a derogatory insult. However, many individuals who enjoy marijuana use it as a term of endearment. So, depending on the circumstance, the remark, "You are such a stoner" is equally likely to receive a response of "Fuck off" as it is "Thanks, you too."

See also **active stoner; antisocial stoner; artistic stoner; casual stoner; enhancement stoner; handy stoner; hungry stoner; intellectual stoner; lazy stoner; paranoid stoner; pothead; social stoner; talkative stoner; violent stoner**

Stoner Film, a subgenre of movies, usually comedies, whose theme or storyline includes overt reference to marijuana use or drug culture. Some examples include: *Super Troopers, Dazed & Confused, Half Baked, How High, Pineapple Express, Harold & Kumar Go To White Castle,*

Dude, Where's My Car?, etc. Stoner films can also include any movie so filled with bad acting and stunted line delivery that it becomes comedy gold. The genre can also be interpreted to include mind-fucks of movies, which would include titles such as: *Being John Malkovich, 2001: A Space Odyssey, Pi, Mullholland Drive, Donnie Darko, Waking Life*, etc. Ultimately, a stoner film is any movie about which someone who smokes weed asks a fellow stoner: "Yeah, but have you ever seen it *high?*"

Straightedge, lifestyle choice of individuals who refrain from alcohol, drugs, and, in some extreme cases, premarital sex. Straightedge individuals occasionally mark themselves on their hands with a big black X, signaling to the rest of the world they are no fun at all. Coming out as a straightedger can be a shocking revelation to friends and family, and many will reject the straightedger out of fear, confusion, general negative feelings of "those types," or just because they find it "icky." As such, straightedgers often find themselves ashamed, alone, and depressed, at which point they find the only friend who never judges them: drugs and alcohol. They are soon reacclimated into society.

See *also* clean; square

Stress, a classification of marijuana that is considered to be of exceptionally low quality and is often used interchangeably with schwag. Weed that falls into this category often contains an excess of stems and seeds and is quite unpleasant to smoke. It is not uncommon for a group of underprivileged stoners to purchase a bag of stress and spend an entire evening complaining how awful it is and how they should never buy it again, only to go out the following evening and do the exact same thing. This could be a result of short-term memory loss or it could just be that stoners love to complain about shit. Especially pot.

See also **schwag**

Strikeout, a game of sorts wherein participants must take a hit of marijuana, down a shot of spirits, and chug a beer before exhaling. Once the act is successfully completed, it is recommended that contestants raise their fists in the air in triumph, although it is not necessary. It is not uncommon for creative players to add any number of additional acts to the game, ranging from doing push-ups to beating the first level of the original Mario Bros. game before exhaling. Regardless of the variation, the game is very similar to tic-tac-toe in that the only winning move is not to play.

See also **highdea**

Strip Clubs, locations, typically in the seedy underbelly of a city, wherein scantily clad men or women shake their moneymakers on a stage and slowly disrobe to the amusement and titillation of the assemblage. When stoners reach the milestone age of eighteen, they are allowed entry into such palaces of sin. As such, several eighteen-year-olds make their birthday plan as follows: get drunk, get stoned, and go to a strip club (this plan is usually announced with much screaming and fist pumping). Upon entry, the stoners are overwhelmed by the "adultness" of it all. It takes about twenty minutes before everyone there realizes they've probably contracted two STDs just from stepping in the place, they're permanently scarred sexually, and they should leave quickly before the experience becomes part of their long-term memory.

© istockphoto / technotr

Tt

Talkative Stoner, a person who is incapable of shutting the fuck up once he or she has ingested cannabis. They are usually under the false impression that they are the first person to have ever gotten high and will regale innocent bystanders with every aspect of their experience. Especially if nobody is listening. If their constant babble becomes irritating (and it will), simply encourage them to continue smoking until they are so baked they can barely stand up, let alone fill everybody in on how much they love *Family Guy*.

See also **active stoner; artistic stoner; casual stoner; enhancement stoner; intellectual stoner; lazy stoner; paranoid stoner; stoner; social stoner**

Thai Stick, a somewhat dated but still kickin' strain of marijuana that originated in Thailand. This is definitely more like one's parents' weed, or even our grandparents'. It was most popular among 1960s and 1970s hippies and draft dodgers. Thai stick is high-quality bud wrapped around a stem and bound with ropelike strands of hemp plant. The end result looks like a little cigar—and it knocks the smoker out of commission longer than an organ solo from The Doors. Thai sticks are rumored to have been dipped in opium, cannabis oil, and even embalming fluid. But those rumors were probably started by embarrassed stoners who didn't want to admit that Thai stick turned them into one-toke jokes.

See also **one-toke joke**

THC, short for tetrahydrocannabinol, a chemical found inside the trichomes of the cannabis plant and known to cause marijuana's enjoyably intoxicating psychotropic effects. Though the biological mechanism by which THC induces euphoria and alters autonomic physical processes such as pain response and appetite are not fully understood, the chemical is one of the safest recreational drugs. One lab study estimates that to self-administer a lethal dose of THC, one would have to smoke 1,500 pounds of cannabis in fourteen minutes—in other words, the exact amount of cannabis one generally desires after reading that estimate. Negative side effects of THC include the inability to differentiate between a sitcom and a drama, eating all of the Pop-Tarts, and the staunching of one's motivation to go out and purchase additional Pop-Tarts.

See also **trichomes**

Thinking, the process by which the brain manages all feelings, impulses, desires, and any humanlike activity not directly involving the five senses, and the way in which people or animals perceive and understand the world around them. Thinking is an unavoidable part of life, but people really dig in to the exercise when stoned. So deep can thought become that stoners disappear into themselves as their eyes roll to the back of their heads. This means the stoner is either experiencing the greatest high of his or her life, or he or she just keeled over and requires immediate medical assistance.

See also **spaced out**

Toke, a popular term in stoner parlance for the act of smoking marijuana. While the word sounds slightly similar to the Tokay gecko, a lizard common to rain forests throughout the world, it is unclear if there is any association between the two. Currently the effects of smoking a gecko remain untested by science.

See also **midnight toker**

Trees, a slang term used to refer to marijuana. The euphemism is especially useful when one wishes to disguise one's intention to get high, as the term can also apply to any number of large plant life that provide breathable oxygen and are not considered illegal to possess, such as weeping willows, birch, oak, etc. Asking someone, "Can I buy some marijuana?" can be very risky. However, asking, "Can I buy some trees?" is much less likely to result in jail time.

Trichomes, tiny bulb-topped filaments that cover the outer surface of cannabis plants and contain the THC that turns boring smoke into a heavenly toke. Often theorized to be a biological defense mechanism designed to make the plant both resilient to harsh weather and unpalatable to herbivores, these narcotic hairs also serve as natural indicators of a marijuana plant's maturity and, ergo, its smokability. Trichomes are naturally occurring evidence that coating one's self with drugs is an exceptionally good self-preservation strategy. No one will ever let weed go extinct. It's something that whales might consider.

See also **THC**

Trip, the period of time between when one consumes a hallucinogenic substance like LSD and when one ceases to see pink elephants dancing around the room. Essentially a miniature vacation from reality. A trip can be broken up into one of two categories: a good one or a bad one. A good trip might find the user floating on a sea of clouds with unicorns galloping in the background. A bad trip is sort of the same thing, only replace the clouds with a sea of laughing troll faces and the unicorns with really creepy clowns.

Tweaking Out, the act of freaking out while under heavy marijuana, mushrooms, or LSD intoxication. Tweaking out can result from several "experiences" the smoker will have while heavily intoxicated. These experiences are typically like walking through a hall of mirrors. Familiar objects become the most mutated things, such as the red candle turning into a laughing maniacal clown. Realizations of the most ordinary kind make a smoker freak out, like that life exists, or that the moon revolves around the earth. Tweaking out may involve spasming of the eyes and neck, cradling in a corner, shaking, covering one's ears, and possibly moaning. Other smokers will attempt to calm the tweaker, first by casually asking, "You OK?" before moving on to the only known cure for tweaking out: a slap across the face and some Ben & Jerry's ice cream.

© istockphoto / aldomurillo

Uu

Uncool, a person, place, thing, or action that is the opposite of cool. This term may seem like a fairly minor insult to the unindoctrinated.

However, for stoners this piece of slang is reserved for only the most undesirable of situations. Like getting caught by the cops, running out of pot, or noticing an instance of bogarting. If one has been called "uncool" by a stoner, the only way to get back in his or her good graces is to offer to pack the next bowl. All will instantly be forgiven.

© istockphoto / senorjackson

See also **cool**

Underwear, any garment worn underneath traditional clothing that is used to create an extra layer of protection and warmth for the most sensitive areas of the human body. Because it's difficult for police or other law enforcement officials to conduct a search of the underwear without risking a sexual harassment lawsuit, it makes for a discreet location to conceal marijuana and other illicit drugs. When employing this method of concealment, please, for the love of God, store the pot in an airtight plastic bag, as swampass and weed do not mix well.

Vaporizer, a method for smoking pot that defies the laws of physics and eliminates a key element in the equation: marijuana plus fire equals high. Rather than being ignited with a flame, pot is heated electronically inside of a partial vacuum to avoid the pesky side effects of standard combustion, like carcinogenic smoke and coughing fits. Vaporizers can be expensive, ranging from just under $100 to around $600 for the coveted Volcano Vaporizer, so only pot-smoking elites are likely to possess one. Some claim a vaporizer takes all the joy out of the smoking experience, as much of the flavor and odor are eliminated in the process. However, this opinion is generally shared only by those who can't afford to smoke out of one.

VCR, an archaic device used for viewing ancient historical documents called movies on equally archaic cartridges called videocassettes. While they have been replaced by DVD players and DVR devices, they have found a second life in the stoner community as discreet hiding places for ganja. Each VCR contains a crevice large enough to house a videocassette, in which one can store minimal quantities of marijuana. One then covers the hole with a small flap to conceal the illicit dope. An entire squad of police officers could pass by it every day and never think to peek inside. One's grandmother, however, is sure to blow one's spot every day at 5:00 when she tapes reruns of *Matlock*.

Vegetarian Joint, a term popularized by the movie *Igby Goes Down* to describe the common practice of vegetarians rolling very thin joints. This is apparently in contrast to meat eaters, who roll big fat blunts. The practice of asking stoners who roll thin joints if they are vegetarians has skyrocketed as a result of the film. Just be careful when asking this question, as, in some circles, being called a vegetarian is the equivalent of being called a narc.

See also **pinner**

Violent Stoner, an oxymoronic term used to describe a breed of stoner that, in theory, becomes uncongenial and violent after smoking cannabis. Not much is known about this variety, as none has ever been observed in the wild. In all likelihood, they do not exist.

See also **antisocial stoner; stoner**

Volcano, an unfortunate gaffe commonly performed by inexperienced smokers whereby, after taking a large hit from a bowl or bong and with their mouth still firmly attached, a smoker begins to cough uncontrollably, sending the burning contents of the bowl erupting toward the sky. This is generally met with nostalgic laughter from experienced smokers, immediately followed by feelings of remorse for the wasted pot and regret that they neglected to take their hit first.

Volcano Vaporizer, a popular brand of vaporizer that has become synonymous with that particular form of drug paraphernalia, similar to Kleenex, Xerox, and Tylenol. The crème de la crème of vaporizers, the Volcano works by heating the herb in a conical base to a preselected temperature and then releasing the vapor into a heatproof bag. The user can then detach the bag and inhale the THC-laden vapor sans potentially harmful by-products commonly found in marijuana smoke. The Volcano is one of the more expensive models on the market, so it is recommended that only quality marijuana be used with the device. Although there is no supporting evidence, it is rumored that the machine will actually sprout legs and skip town at the first sign of schwag, shake, or any pot that has been "stepped on."

Wacky Tobaccy, a derogatory term often used by old people, police officers, and anyone who has never smoked pot to refer to marijuana. The term is derived from the fact that marijuana shares several similarities with tobacco (they are both dry, smokable, and often rolled into cigarettes), combined with the fact that it makes the user act strange, disoriented, or "wacky." Also, the two words almost kind of rhyme. Whenever anyone suggests that the group smoke some "wacky tobacco," it is best either to run away as quickly as possible or knock the person unconscious with a blunt object and tie them up for questioning, as the person is most certainly a narc. Or a douche. In either case the beating is justified.

Wake 'N' Bake, the process by which a person wakes up in the morning and, rather than leaping out of bed to greet the day, opts instead to stay in bed and get high. This activity will often take precedence over going to the bathroom, walking the dog, eating breakfast, job hunting, or any number of other common morning rituals. While sporadic participation in this practice is harmless, there is the potential risk that, if done consistently, one can forget what it's like *not* to be stoned.

Waking Life, the experience of being alive, awaking in the morning (or early afternoon, for some stoners), eating breakfast, maybe showering, brushing teeth, dressing, going out into the world, interacting with other humans, learning, teaching, thinking, living—the polar opposite of being asleep (though the two are often mistaken for each other). When sober, waking life can seem boring, normal, unspectacular, completely ordinary, etc. When stoned, waking life can appear scary, fun, silly, unserious, satirical, surreal, absurd, and totally sweet. People who get stoned while performing the normal activities of their day are following the script of Michael Douglas's character in *Wonder Boys*, and that includes many readers of this book. It requires a high level of functionality, a skill set most stoners lack, and is not recommended for anyone who does any job that requires the use of safety glasses.

Wasted, a state of being achieved through overindulgence in marijuana, often in combination with other substances, that is beyond high, stoned, baked, or even ripped. This state is usually achieved when the rational portion of a smoker's brain loses a battle to the portion that really wants to keep taking gravity bong hits. The latter portion has little concern for the well-being of its host. Scientists believe this area of the brain is also responsible for drunk-dialing ex-lovers, lighting the wrong end of the cigarette, walking home at 4:00 A.M. in the rain without a coat, and watching countless hours of *Adult Swim*.

Water, a chemical compound necessary for human life that is created by combining two parts hydrogen with one part oxygen. The average human requires around six glasses of the life-sustaining liquid when not smoking pot. However, that number skyrockets while under the influence and can approach infinity depending on the harshness of the bud being smoked. When used properly, water can also serve as a medium for cooling marijuana smoke before it is inhaled into the lungs, although this process creates a foul-smelling by-product

© istockphoto / morkeman

known as bong water. In instances when there is enough available water only to fill a bong or use as a means of hydration but not both, one may be tempted to use it for smoking purposes and then drink the bong water. This is a terrible idea, but for the sake of hilarity one should never intervene if a friend attempts this practice.

See also bong water

Water Bottle, a hollow plastic container used for transporting the life-sustaining substance known as water. While relatively inexpensive and unassuming, it is arguably the single most important piece of equipment any stoner can have in his or her arsenal, as dehydration is a common side effect of smoking weed, and other methods for transporting water, like cups or one's hands, are far less efficient and prone to spillage. Also, the water bottle is one of the only means of transporting water that can be transformed into a smoking device when times are tough. Once it has been cannibalized for smoking purposes it can never be used as a water receptacle again, so one should try all other avenues before resorting to this extreme measure.

See also water bottle bong

Water Bottle Bong, a smoking apparatus generally built only when one is alone at home and at a complete loss for any other means from which to get high and/or happens to be exceedingly bored. The device is constructed from a hollow household item, such as a pen or marker, attached to a plastic water bottle. For the sake of economics or as a direct result of extreme laziness, the bowl head is usually constructed out of tinfoil. Using a cutting tool, the hopeful smoker makes a hole in the bottle, affixes the makeshift bowl onto the hollow object, and inserts said object into the hole. Filling the bottom of the bottle with water will act as a cooling agent and add legitimacy to the bong. However, nothing can change the fact that the user is still smoking pot alone in his or her room out of a plastic bottle.

See also **water bottle**

Weed, arguably the most popular euphemism used to refer to marijuana by modern men and women. While the word carries a negative connotation in horticultural circles (e.g., "These damn weeds are killing my azaleas!"), it could not be used more lovingly in the pot-smoking world (e.g., "If it weren't for weed, I don't think I'd bother getting up in the morning.").

See also **every entry in this book**

Weed Tea, a drink created by steeping marijuana in boiling water for an extended period to time. Because THC is not especially water soluble, the psychedelic properties of the resulting brew are fairly mild. To increase the potency of the tea, one can add ingredients with high fat contents like milk, butter, or vegetable oil. On its own, weed tea is not very appetizing, so one can add flavor enhancers like honey, sugar, or tea leaves. Of course, one could also abandon the notion of weed tea altogether and simply smoke the stuff, but that wouldn't be nearly as fun.

White Widow, a notoriously potent, high-yield strain of cannabis named for the abundant number of THC-rich trichomes that cover its exterior, giving the plant its trademark frosted appearance. Originally developed in Amsterdam, and winner of the 1995 Cannabis Cup, White Widow is actually a crossbreed of the Indian indica strain and the Brazilian sativa strain. Infamous for its pure, intoxicating strength, Widow is the only type of marijuana known for making Superman forget to change out of his costume before going back to *The Daily Planet*, and everyone there was like, "Hey, Superman. Are you high?" And Superman was like, "Nope." (giggle) "Just stopping evil is all!" and people said, "Oh. Okay." And Superman was like, "You ever notice how when you write 'OK,' it looks like a little man who fell over and now he needs to be saved? Like, what if I saved him, you guys? Huh? What would happen? You know? Like, to the world?"

See also OK

Woo Blunt, a normal cigar-shaped marijuana receptacle that has been enhanced with cocaine. One should only roll a woo blunt with the express knowledge of everyone in the group, and never discreetly for one's own sick pleasure. Even when done openly, this practice is often frowned upon by many stoners who feel that pot is good enough on its own and doesn't need the help of cocaine, its distant cousin twice removed.

© istockphoto / AVTG

Woods, The, an outside location populated by trees, bugs, birds, and other assorted nature; a popular location to toke up in due to its isolated and cop-free surroundings. The woods are also a profound place to get high, especially when weed is combined with more powerful hallucinogens, as trees begin telling stoners to please not cut them down and chirping crickets begin to sound like Sgt. Pepper's Lonely Hearts Club Band. This can lead to a stoner tweaking out, spontaneously declaring him or herself to be a vegan, or hugging a tree. There is no known cure for this debilitating disease, except time and prayer.

Xenophobia, a state of being similar to paranoia but instead of a broad distrust of the universe at large, the subject's irrational fear is directed specifically at people and cultures different from his or her own. Among pot smokers, this most commonly manifests as a general negative attitude toward the quality of marijuana from areas of the world a smoker has not yet visited. For example, a Canadian smoker might scoff at Amsterdam weed and subsequently point out how awesome bud from various regions of Canada is. Some speculate that Aesop's famous fable *The Fox and the Grapes* is actually a reference to this phenomenon and was originally titled *The Stoner and the Bag of Greek Schwag*.

Xeric, a term used by overeducated potheads to describe marijuana that is exceptionally dry. Premium bud is usually a little sticky to the touch and should never turn to dust in one's hands. The term has yet to catch on among the larger pot-smoking community, primarily because it is impossible to use it in a sentence without sounding like a pretentious dick.

Yellow Submarine, either the tenth studio album released by the Beatles, or another name for weed. Despite Paul McCartney's claim that the song "Yellow Submarine" was written as a children's song, stoners all over the world entertain themselves by deconstructing the lyrics to find the song's hidden meanings.

Yerba, a slang term for marijuana that comes from the name of the yerba mate tree, which can be found in South American rain forests. A drink brewed from its leaves has almost as many health benefits as medical marijuana.

Zen, a state of being achieved through excessive marijuana use that is generally described as an extreme feeling of contentedness. The term derives from a sect of Buddhism whose followers practice meditation as a means for achieving enlightenment. While the average pot smoker is not necessarily seeking spiritual oneness, the similarities between stoners and Buddhist monks is startling. Replace the orange robes with an orange hoodie and the word "om" with the word "um" and nobody would ever know the difference.

Zoinks!, an exclamation of surprise, confusion, annoyance, or relief made by the animated character Shaggy on the "popular" Hanna-Barbera cartoon *Scooby-Doo, Where Are You!* Despite Shaggy's iconic status within the pot-smoking community, the slang term has yet to catch on in the real world. This could be due to the real world's lack of ghosts, mummies, and other monsters hiding inside suits of armor ready to jump out and scare hapless victims, thus eliminating the need for the use of the term.

Zong, a bong with a Z-shaped tube that doubles its capacity for smoke. Allows a four-foot bong to fit in a two-foot space. Great for bus drivers, hikers, and flight attendants. Rumored to have been invented by Thomas Edison. However, the only evidence to substantiate this are sixteen primitive recordings filled with nothing but giggling and extended periods of contemplative silence.

Zonked, a term used to describe being really tired, stoned, and generally spent. Once one has achieved this state, there's no coming back without the proper application of time and sleep. One could try smoking more pot in a misguided attempt to get so high that one actually comes back around full circle and sobers up. However, if this does succeed, the ensuing down leaves the smoker so zonked he or she is likely to sleep for eighteen straight hours.

See also **passing out**

Zoo, a place where no one can tell that one is high, because everyone else is just as busy gawking at animals and saying stupid shit. In a tangentially related note, polar bears' fur is actually *clear*? Whoahhhhh.

Appendix:
The Hungry Stoner's
Guide to Munchies

Auntie Anne's, a food court staple and favorite location for grand-mothers to take their grandchildren. It's also an irresistible spot for a munchies fix. The menu is almost unfairly stacked, appealing to the salt- and sugar-inclined. Here are just some of the items available: pep-peroni pretzel, cinnamon sugar pretzel, almond pretzel, pretzel dog. The dips don't help: cheese, marinara, caramel, sweet mus-tard. And for the indecisive: the dip sampler. If pot is ever legal-ized, Auntie Anne's stock is pre-dicted to skyrocket.

© istockphoto / Sage78

Bacon, the single greatest food known to man. In its most basic form, bacon is a thin strip of pig flesh that has been cured with salt and then dried, smoked, or served fresh. Due to its high salt content and ease of preparation, bacon has earned a welcome place in the list of quality munchies among stoners. Independent of weedophile culture, the food experienced an unprecedented rise in popularity in the 1980s and '90s thanks in part to a protein-centric way of eating called the Atkins Diet. Currently there are scores of cookbooks, fan clubs, and websites devoted to the food, with celebrity chefs like Bobby Flay even hopping on the bacon band-wagon. The sudden rise in popularity is clear evidence that the rest of the world has started to realize a simple fact that pot smokers have known for centuries—bacon makes everything better.

© istockphoto / Floortje

Bagel Bites, mass-produced frozen snack foods that resemble vari-eties of pizza resting atop miniature bagels, probably because that's exactly what they are. Because they can be microwaved in a matter of minutes and are fairly difficult to screw up, the stoner community has embraced them as a reliable munchie for times when one is willing to forgo the instant gratification of chips and raw cookie dough in favor of a warm, tasty treat.

See also pizza

Banana Stand, a purveyor of frozen bananas to legions of over-heated stoners that exists solely in the *Arrested Development* universe. The location spawned the song "Big Yellow Joint," a ditty recorded by Jimmy Jane in the 1970s to pay homage to the Bluth Frozen Banana stand and its iconic resemblance to a yellow marijuana cigarette. The banana stand served as a meeting place for stoners looking to get high while enjoying a delicious frozen treat. When it isn't being pushed into the harbor or burned to the ground, there is always money in it.

Beer, the beverage of choice for most humans aged sixteen and older when eating pizza, peanuts, pretzels, hanging amongst friends, or trying to get drunk. Beer is a hallmark of American culture, a companion during adolescence, college, and beyond. Beer is also the companion drug to marijuana. Alcohol and marijuana are often compared when pundits are debating legalizing marijuana, but more importantly, beer is a delicious beverage to accompany the pot-smoking experience. It's important not to confuse the beer bottle with the bong, though, or else a pot smoker will drink the worst-tasting beer of his or her life.

Ben & Jerry's, a Vermont-based ice cream, fro-yo, and sorbet company and favorite munchies choice of the stoner. Grocery store clerks know when their customers are getting ready to get high, because they're the ones who, without a cart, arrive at the checkout line balancing an armful of Ben & Jerry's ice cream, keeping it stacked only by allowing their forward momentum to help them reach the counter, at which point they stop and the buckets of Ben & Jerry's ice cream come tumbling forward. Stoners are known to pick flavors based on Ben & Jerry's names, which include AmeriCone Dream (so named for TV's Stephen Colbert) and Phish Food (so named for the band). Other flavors include such titles as Half-Baked, Jamaican Me Crazy, and Imagine Whirled Peace, proving the company knows its customer base consists largely of loyal, pun-loving pot smokers.

See also ice cream; toast cream

Cereal, the most basic, easy, and delicious breakfast food, which can also be eaten, by the sophisticates in society, for lunch or dinner. Cereal is a great choice for binge eating, depending on which cereal is purchased, as it can be extremely delicious while remaining relatively not unhealthy. This all goes down the toilet, however, when sugary cereals are introduced into the mix. Stoners are capable of going through entire boxes of Frosted Flakes without so much as stopping to play the word search on the back of the box. The only saving grace is that after twelve such binges, a stoner will have enough UPC codes to collect a free Tony the Tiger stuffed animal.

Cheetos, a branded cornmeal product caked in imitation cheese and brought to the marketplace by an anthropomorphic cartoon feline, Chester Cheetah. Among the least nutritious foods produced, Cheetos are nevertheless a staple of the munchie binge. Stoners susceptible to downing an entire bag of Cheetos will inevitably develop the Cheetos hangover, characterized by pained moaning, orange puke, and the promise to "never eat Cheetos again." This promise will last until whenever the smoker decides to get high again and will subsequently be forgotten.

Chicken Wings, a late-night snack of choice for smokers. This may be because they're easily accessible, inexpensive, and just straight-up delicious. Remember those empty Chinese-food containers littering the floor of a pot smoker's lair? They used to have chicken wings in them.

Chocolate Milk, ordinary milk that achieves its full munchie potential thanks to the addition of chocolate syrup. Stoners are particularly fond of the drink's simplicity, as they tend to shun any food with more than two ingredients. The typical technique used to make the concoction is to fill a glass with milk, squirt syrup into said glass, and stir.

© istockphoto / segovia_r

If one is lacking a glass, one can simply fill the mouth with milk, squirt syrup into said mouth, and shake one's head around to mix, a method popularized by the '90s sitcom *Step by Step*.

Cookie, a dessert consisting of varying levels of sugar, butter, flour, eggs, and additional ingredients like nuts and chocolate to produce everything from the humble sugar cookie to the hulking oatmeal raisin. Under normal circumstances, the average human can consume two or three cookies before becoming full. This number, however, does not apply to humans who have recently smoked pot. For such individuals the maximum number of cookies is nearly without limit. Especially if the cookies are double stuffed, triple chocolate, or made by Girl Scouts.

© istockphoto / burwellphotography

See also **cookie dough**

Cookie Dough, a combination of raw materials that, when exposed to high temperatures, magically becomes cookies. While cookie dough is by no means complicated to make from scratch, it can be a bit of a challenge for those under the influence. Many popular cookie companies, clearly aware of the plight of the average stoner, began selling cookie dough in refrigerated tubes for easy slicing and baking. Later, those same companies made it even easier by creating tear-away, prepackaged blocks. Focus groups have shown that the new packaging makes little difference to the average stoner, as the vast majority had never considered baking the dough in the first place, preferring to eat it raw.

See also cookies

Cream Soda Surprise, a stoner treat. When vanilla ice cream and flat vanilla cream soda are combined, something wonderful happens. After they're mixed together, one sip cures the marijuana user's cotton mouth with a rush of vanilla sweetness. The flat soda creates a smooth texture, enticing the drinker for a second glass. The process of making the concoction—flattening soda, scooping, and stirring—brings a healthy balance of work and reward to the drug user's experience. The surprise is that only stoners seem to like it.

See also pop

Deep Fryer, essentially the stoner's best friend. This cooking device heats oil up to between 300 and 450 degrees Fahrenheit so that the hungry stoner can infuse various food items like chicken wings, potatoes, mozzarella sticks, pickles, and even ice cream and candy bars with delicious oil. The appliance creates a bit of a paradox, wherein it is an essential tool for creating the majority of munchie staples, but it is arguably the most dangerous tool known to man to attempt to operate when stoned. For this reason, it is always wise to have a nonsmoking friend act as chef for the evening. This person can also act as a sober liaison should somebody need to talk to the police for any reason.

Delivery, the process by which food is prepared at a restaurant and then brought directly to the customer, because the consumer of said food is too lazy or too stoned (or both) to come pick it up. This can be an invaluable service for times when everyone in the smoking circle neglected to purchase munchies or a preplanned cooking session becomes far too risky a venture. Generally there is a premium for this service in the form of a tip for the underpaid teenager who handles the delivery. Be nice to these people, because if one keeps getting stoned and spending so much money on pizza, one is but a misstep away from wearing one's own delivery uniform.

See also **drive-through**

Denny's, a chain restaurant known for being open twenty-four hours a day and for serving breakfast, lunch, and dinner at all times. This makes Denny's a popular location for the 2 A.M. munchies run. While Denny's food can be described as consistently average, this is of no consequence to food-craving pot smokers who down Grand Slam meals as if they're water.

Domino's, a nationwide pizza chain which makes either the world's best pizza or the world's worst pizza, depending on whom one asks. The company once promised pizza in less than thirty minutes or it was free, but it clearly underestimated the demands of a nation of hungry, impatient potheads. In the years leading up to the discontinuation of the promotion, there were several car accidents allegedly as a result of delivery drivers racing to make their thirty-minute deadline. It's also possible that the chain simply got tired of stoned customers calling five minutes after placing their order, demanding free pizza. To them the few minutes seemed like several hours.

See also **delivery**

Doritos, a popular brand of chip with numerous flavor varieties, all of which seem to be coated with a magical powder that, when combined with THC, makes them irresistible to humans (and certain breeds of dogs). Unsuspecting potheads should be warned of tragically eating themselves to death during a particularly violent binge-eating episode.

See also potato chips

Double Down, KFC's much-hyped sandwich, released in 2010, which features two thick and juicy boneless white-meat chicken fillets, two pieces of bacon, two melted slices of Monterey jack and pepper jack cheese and special Colonel's Sauce. Also known as the star of a pot smoker's wet dream.

Drive-Through, a popular feature ubiquitous to fast-food restaurants like McDonald's, Taco Bell, and Burger King that allows customers to pull their cars up alongside the restaurant, yell their order at a menu with a microphone, and pay for their food and pick it up at a window farther down the line. This is especially useful for stoners, as it eliminates much of the troublesome in-person interaction that can be difficult to accomplish with a straight face while high. Unfortunately, access to the drive-through is generally off-limits to pedestrians and cyclists, so financially challenged stoners must suck it up and risk running into a local police officer or high school principal while standing in line. Fortunately, that's why hoodies were invented.

See also value menu

Easy Mac, a substance that might be classified as food but is more accurately a conglomerate of calories, cheese molecules, and cardboard resembling the popular pasta dish macaroni and cheese. That aside, it is arguably one of the most sought-after snacks after the consumption of marijuana. Pot's tendency to enhance flavors is one possible explanation for this paradox, but the more likely answer is that, at the end of the day, a microwave is infinitely safer to operate while high than a stove will ever be.

See also **microwave**

Flying J, a service stop on highways across America which is open for most late-night needs and always comes into sight just as a stoned driver is certain he or she is going to run out of gas. Flying Js (mostly because of the name) are a favorite late-night spot for the stoner who has been awake all night driving cross-country following Roger Waters on tour. They're good spots for picking up supplies such as doughnuts, Red Bull, and coffee. There is about zero risk of being questioned, no matter how much someone smells like weed, as stoners are almost always the least shady people there, even when only the clerk is present.

Food, caloric intake meant to sustain the bodily functions of life. Most things stoners eat do qualify as food: fruit, pasta, peanut butter, ice cream, pizza, etc. However, stoners push the boundaries of what qualifies as food constantly. For example, Cheez Whiz on tortilla: food or not food? Experts disagree. Nevertheless, food or what is almost food is one of the best things about getting high. How food tastes increases exponentially once inebriated. As a result, presmoking rituals may include trips to local grocery stores to stock up on edibles.

See *also* munchies

French Fries, a dish that consists of potatoes cut into thin strips and fried in oil to produce a crisp, golden-brown finger food perfect for dipping into various flavor enhancers like ketchup, barbecue sauce, milkshakes, and (in some forward-thinking countries) mayonnaise.

Making them from scratch can be wildly dangerous in the best of circumstances, so it is usually advised that those in search of a French fry fix seek out their nearest fast-food restaurant or supermarket freezer section while under the influence. It is a well-documented fact that burning-hot oil will kill a stoner's buzz on contact.

© istockphoto / Alst

Fritos, a corn-chip snack that comes in a variety of flavors but one instantly recognizable shape. The tiny, warped rectangle is the Fritos's style and has been since the outset. It's so tiny that bagfuls of Fritos can be put down without stoned eaters realizing the cholesterol, saturated fat, and sodium intake they're indulging in. This in turn leads to the Fritos hangover: flatulence, pimples, and terrible, terrible regret.

See also **potato chips**

Frozen Chicken Nuggets, fun-sized breaded chicken portions designed for easy home preparation. These scrumptious poultry num-nums were developed in the 1950s as part of an academic project undertaken by a food scientist at Cornell University. If the project was to find the ultimate method of simultaneously enticing and infuriating a nation of starving stoners, one can only assume the scientist in question received an A with a smiley face next to it. Frozen chicken nuggets represent the cutting edge of delayed gratification. Factoring in oven preheat time, they cook thirty times longer than a Pop-Tart and ten times longer than a Hot Pocket, but flavorwise trump both. Add dipping sauce, and the deliciousness quotient is off the scale. It's, therefore, recommended that one initiate nugget prep prior to smoking up. Otherwise, one is liable to get impatient to the point of microwaving the nuggets, which always ends in disappointment. Shriveled, leathery disappointment.

See also **microwave**

Frozen Raspberries, small, squishy, red fruit stored at a temperature below thirty-two degrees Fahrenheit for the purposes of storage, transportation, and consumption. Frozen raspberries are one of a handful of fruits designed for the naturalist stoner, the vegan stoner, or the health-conscious stoner. Once they're tried, they become the best stoner food available. They're tasty, interesting, sweet, and fairly healthy. Regrettably their caloric value is very low, meaning that even after going through three bags of frozen raspberries, the stoner is still looking for food. There's one other problem. While delicious in nature, frozen raspberries leave eaters with red-stained fingers, which in turn leads to a red-stained shirt, couch, remote control, and face.

Funyuns, a crunchy onion-flavored food item produced by Frito-Lay that has about as much real onion in it as this book has real marijuana. The snack appears in the stoner film *Half Baked* as the final item on an extensive list of essential munchies dictated by Jim Breuer, thus securing its place in weedophile history. The list included sour cream and onion chips, dip, beef jerky, peanut butter, Häagen-Dazs ice cream bars, chocolate, popcorn, graham crackers, little marshmallows and little chocolate bars (for s'mores), celery, grape jelly, Cap'n Crunch with the little Crunch Berries, pizzas with everything on 'em, and a whole lotta water. This is the only documented instance in which a request for Funyuns was not the oddest item on a list.

Gatorade, a popular brand of sports drink enjoyed by athletes looking to rehydrate after hours of intense physical exertion. It is also popular among stoners looking to rehydrate after hours of intense couch sitting and bong ripping. Developed by a group of researchers at the University of Florida in 1965, the drink is affectionately named after the school's football team, the Florida Gators. The substance is superior to water in that it contains sugar, yellow, and electrolytes. Nobody is exactly sure what electrolytes are, but the general consensus is that they are good.

Grilled Cheese, a common snack when one is spontaneously hit with the munchies, perhaps because all of the ingredients (butter, cheese, and white bread) are usually on hand. Can easily be made into a variation using marijuana by cooking the weed in butter before sautéing the bread. Be forewarned: Doing so may bring on more munchies instead of curing the original onset.

See also **sliced bread**

Hot Pockets, pastry treats filled with cheese, meat, vegetables, and other assorted foodlike items which can be, and often are, microwaved for a near-instant munchies fix. Hot Pockets come in breakfast, lunch, and dinner varieties, so they can accommodate any stoned occasion and provide a constant flow of cheese, flavor, and cholesterol to the body.

See also microwave

Hummus, a popular munchie among hipster stoners. The basic version consists of ground-up chickpeas mixed with garlic, tahini, and olive oil. It is prized for its versatility, as it can be spread on bread, pita chips, bagels, fruit or vegetables, or simply eaten raw by dipping one's fingers into the tub and licking them clean. The last option is disgusting and should be employed only when nobody else involved in the smoking session is in a position to observe and subsequently judge.

Hunger, a sensation that occurs in the human body when the stomach increases the levels of the hormone ghrelin found in its lining to alert the hands that it's time to make a sandwich. Certain activities can stimulate this reaction, such as fasting, exercising, smoking marijuana, and standing downwind of bakeries.

Ice Cream, a combination of dairy products and natural or artificial flavorings which, when combined and frozen, create a magical, heavenly experience that rivals sex, skydiving, and the effects of various drugs. Frequently consumed as a post-pot-smoking munchie, its cooling properties are especially useful for combating the negative effects hot marijuana smoke can have on the human mouth. If allowed to melt in the mouth before swallowing, it can help alleviate cotton mouth. Also, it is a necessary ingredient in other popular munchie concoctions like toast cream and milkshakes.

See also **milkshake; toast cream**

International House of Pancakes (IHOP), fast-food restaurants featuring breakfast all day and night. The chain claims to serve more than 700 million pancakes every year: 1 million to families with small children—a key demographic—and the other 699 million to mysteriously famished and suspiciously giggly college students at 3 A.M. Eating at the International House of Pancakes will surely prepare any would-be world traveler for the variety of cuisines found in other countries. The curious customer can order Danish or Swedish crepes, French toast, or that truly international culinary favorite: the Rooty Tooty Fresh 'n' Fruity.

KFC/Pizza Hut/Taco Bell, a holy trinity of fast-food restaurants which, when the stars and planets align just right, can all be found under one central roof. To fully understand the feeling a hungry stoner experiences when coming across such a goldmine of munchie options, one must try to imagine what it would feel like to find a $100 bill on the ground on the way to work, arrive and discover the office has been closed for the day, and solve world hunger while walking in the park on a sunny afternoon. The feeling experienced in that scenario equates to about .25 percent of the happiness experienced by the aforementioned hungry stoner.

© istockphoto / tonyoquias

See also **Double Down**

Lobster with Bud Butter,

a bottom-dwelling crustacean most commonly boiled, steamed, or grilled and then dipped in butter that has been infused with the mind-expanding powers of the cannabis plant. Lobster can be quite expensive, as can the process of making pot butter, so this combination is generally reserved for pot smokers with more expensive tastes than the average stoner. Those with limited means should avoid this extravagant meal, as indulging even once could instantly take all the joy out of eating humble rasta pasta or pot brownies.

See also **pot butter**

Microwave, a common kitchen appliance invented by Percy Spencer in 1945 used for the cooking of food. The device works by bombarding food molecules with microwave radiation to rapidly heat the food, a process that is probably harmless to humans. The microwave is easy to operate, works in a matter of minutes, and requires absolutely no monitoring on the part of the user. Guess who likes that idea. The stoner community has been using the microwave as the primary means for munchie preparation since its inception, preferring it to more dangerous cooking methods like baking, sautéing, roasting, and anything that involves more thought than hitting buttons and waiting patiently.

© istockphoto / 2happy

See also **Easy Mac; Hot Pockets**

Milkshake, a combination of milk and ice cream that is mixed together in a blender, poured into a glass, and slurped through a straw. The milkshake makes for an excellent munchie for several reasons. First and foremost, it is delicious. Second, its deliciousness is increased exponentially by adding any number of common kitchen staples like chocolate syrup, peanut butter, or whipped cream. And last but not least, the fact that it is in liquid form makes it easy to ingest quickly and can also help to alleviate the symptom of cotton mouth. Smokers should take caution while enjoying a milkshake, as there is a slight risk of developing brief but excruciating pain localized within the forehead. Of course this can easily be avoided by enjoying the milkshake slowly. However, everyone knows such a feat would be impossible.

Munchies (Foodstuffs), a diverse line of Frito-Lay snack mixes clearly targeted at a less-than-sober, crunch-jonesing demographic. Deftly divided into three separate varieties—"Cheese Fix," "Flamin' Hot," and "Totally Ranch"—Munchies cater directly to every form of pot-inspired tummy ailment, ranging from cheese withdrawal to ranch deficiency. Note that Canada, a country far more open to the smoke 'n' toke antics of herb-frenzied consumers, boasts two additional Munchies phyla: "BBQ" and "Reduced Fat." Unsurprisingly, Frito-Lay was forced to discontinue "Kid's Mix" Munchies—not because seven-year-olds aren't smoking weed, but rather because their bleeding-heart parents are forcing them to munch organic.

Nachos, a culinary delight associated with Tex-Mex cuisine. Nachos were originally created from the humble combination of cheese and tortillas but have morphed to include everything from salsa and ground beef to catfish, pickles, sweet potatoes, and pretty much anything that one has lying around. In fact, scientists have yet to discover a food item that does not work with nachos, although they came close with the combination of lamb, ice cream, and rakfisk. Nachos are most commonly enjoyed either as a lunch replacement or in stoner food celebrations.

Nutella, considered by many to be one of the most delectable condiments in existence. Nutella is a mixture of skim milk, hazelnuts, and cocoa. Pairs well with bananas, toasted bread, and weed, when spread between two crackers and baked (often referred to as a Nutella Firecracker).

Odwalla, a company founded in the mid-'80s in California which produces the best stoner-approved juices and smoothies money can buy. Unlike competitors who stick with a single fruit per container, the folks at Odwalla choose to throw just about anything they can think of into the blender to produce flavors like Red Rhapsody, containing raspberries, strawberries, and pomegranates with some beets and tomatoes thrown in for good measure. While some stoners have attempted to recreate the magic of Odwalla in their own kitchens with assorted produce, a Magic Bullet, and some free time, it's best to leave that sort of thing to the professionals.

Oranges, citrus fruits which can serve a number of uses for an industrious stoner. First and foremost, they are a portable munchie which can be easily carried in a backpack, large pocket, or hand and eaten at the smoker's leisure. The peel also has mystical properties which can turn dried-up pot into sticky icky if one tosses peel and weed into a sealed container for a few hours. Unfortunately, its transformative properties apply only to pot. Keeping orange peels in one's room will not improve one's life. It will make one's room smell like oranges, though, which isn't half-bad.

Peanut Butter, a creamy delight made of ground peanuts, salt, and other stuff. The main ingredient in nutcrackers, a beloved marijuana snack made by spreading peanut butter between two crackers, then sprinkling it with weed before making it into a sandwich.

Pickles, a condiment, snack, or meal, depending on how stoned one is. Pickles begin life as humble cucumbers but achieve their true flavor potential with the help of vinegar, salt, garlic, dill, and time. Pickles come in a number of varieties ranging from crisp, garlicky kosher dills to sweet-and-sour bread and butter chips. Similar to pairings of various foods with wine, some believe the type of pickle one should enjoy varies depending on the type of pot being smoked. Gherkins, for example, are best enjoyed with a gram of 2002 Northern Lights.

Pizza, possibly the greatest food ever invented. Pizza consists of bread, tomato sauce, and cheese, with any choice of toppings for an additional ninety-nine cents. Pizza is the rare food that can be delivered, picked up, or baked at home. It also tastes good, from low-end brands to the highest delicacy. While pizza is obviously a staple of the stoner's experience, so too are pizza boxes. What that means is that on rare occasions, a postslumber stoner may wander into the kitchen craving just one more piece. When the marijuana gods are smiling, the stoner will hopefully open the pizza box cover and, as if a golden light beams out from inside, find one last piece remaining. That last piece, cold, stale, and lifeless, is still the greatest-tasting single piece of pizza in history.

See also pizza sandwich

Pizza Sandwich, arguably one of the least creative munchies ever developed by potheads. The pizza sandwich is simply two pieces of pizza stacked on top of one another to create a superslice. Twice as filling as a single slice and 25 percent more portable, the resulting sandwich is the perfect marriage of ingenuity and a false sense of accomplishment.

See also pizza

Pop, the correct way to refer to any carbonated drink that isn't seltzer or tonic water if one is from one part of a country, and a really stupid way to refer to any carbonated drink that isn't seltzer or tonic water if one is from some other part of the country. Pop is an essential item to have on hand when smoking large quantities of marijuana, as it can be used to alleviate cotton mouth or stave off an impending coughing fit. It also happens to be delicious, but this fact often goes unnoticed by particularly wasted stoners chugging it faster than their taste buds can register the potpourri of flavors.

Pop-Tarts, a landmark achievement in American food history, combining a sugary pastry with jam filling, frosting, and crunchy warmth to create a flavor paradise. Pop-Tarts are delicious and easy to consume for the stoner, as they can be eaten either toasted or cold. Pop-Tarts are not only a staple of the American food culture, they're also downright patriotic, as the U.S. military briefly dropped them over Afghanistan in 2001 during the initial invasion of the country. That means the stoner who buys them supports America, not only because Pop Tarts are essential to national security operations, apparently, but also because they have come to represent the obesity epidemic that has taken America by storm.

Popcorn, regular corn that can achieve its full potential only after the application of heat and artificial butter topping. It is an exceptionally popular stoner food, because it meets all of the necessary munchie requirements: It's salty, delicious, there's lots of it, and it's microwavable. The only proper method for consuming popcorn is to take large fistfuls and shove them into one's mouth hole repeatedly.

Pot Brownies, a popular baked good that has been prepared with a secret ingredient that, given the name of the dessert, is not a secret at all. Often called "special" brownies, the treat is made by following a traditional recipe for brownies but substituting pot butter in place of regular butter. Once finished, the confection appears identical to a normal brownie to the naked eye. Any differences will not be discovered until about a half hour or so after one has ingested the brownie. When consuming pot brownies it is very important to have additional munchies on hand that do not contain any marijuana. Otherwise, the temptation to consume more brownies could be unbearable.

See also pot butter; pot oil

Pot Butter, an essential ingredient when cooking with cannabis. It consists of ordinary butter that has been infused with the mind-enhancing substance THC through the application of heat, time, and grim determination. When baked into snacks like cookies and brownies, the time it takes for the THC to be absorbed in the stomach and then permeate the blood stream can be significantly longer than when pot is smoked. If one does not feel the effects within thirty minutes of consumption, it is wise to be patient and resist the urge to continue eating them. The experience is worth the wait.

See also **pot oil**

Pot Cake, simply put, is cake with pot in it. While this application may seem like an ingenious idea for stoner birthday parties, it can be difficult to section the finished product into uniform individual servings. In theory, each person should get a single slice of cake, but how does one define a slice? Most people would judge it as two slanted cuts meeting at a single point to create a piece that is approximately two inches wide at the end, but what if one's friend pulls a Garfield, cuts a thin sliver out, and bogarts the rest of the cake? Better to avoid the problem entirely and stick with cupcakes.

© istockphoto / AdShooter

See also **pot butter; pot oil**

Pot Oil, similar to pot butter, but made instead with any type of edible oil. THC is fat-soluble, so oils with higher fat contents like coconut and palm are better suited for this culinary adventure. In its most basic form, pot oil is created by heating oil and sautéing the desired amount of bud in said oil for an extended period of time (usually from thirty minutes to an hour). Once strained, the resulting oil can be drizzled on pasta, bread, or directly into the mouth. However, only two of these applications could be considered "good" ideas.

See also **pot butter**

Potato Chips, a munchie staple consisting of paper-thin potato slices that have been deep fried and coated with salt or a number of other flavorings like garlic, pepper, sour cream, vinegar, and various herbs. The invention of the delicacy is generally attributed to Saratoga chef George Crum who, in the mid-1800s, served them to a disgruntled customer complaining his French fries were too thick. While this fanciful tale makes for a good story, it is far more likely that Crum just got stoned one evening and started throwing different foods into the deep fryer to see what would happen. In general, that explanation applies to all deep-fried munchies, but most specifically pork rinds, deep-fried Oreos, and the Awesome Blossom.

See also **Doritos; Fritos; Pringles**

Pringles, tube-packaged potato-ish chip with the longtime marketing slogan "Once you pop, you can't stop." It's a fate the pot smoker is doomed to repeat over and over. The chip's combination of crispiness, saltiness, and flavor options leaves the marijuana-impaired consumer little self-control. Pringles did build in one consumer-protection measure, though. Their long, oval-shaped container leaves eaters at risk of developing Pringles hands (Solanum manus). Just like getting a hand caught in a pickle jar, Pringles hands leaves the can affixed to the appendage and unremovable. The only known cure is a hospital visit and scissors. Once the can is removed, the stoner will indulge in licking his hands until every morsel of salt has been removed and fully treasured.

See also potato chips; salt

Rakfisk, a regional dish found in areas of Norway consisting of a fish that has been cured and allowed to ferment for several months. Deemed the antimunchie by some stoners, rakfisk is one of only a handful of foods that the degree to which a person would need to be high in order to crave it exceeds the limitations of the human body. Other examples of such foods include casu marzu (maggot-ridden cheese), balut (partially developed duck or chicken egg), and baby mice wine (exactly what it sounds like).

Ramen, a Japanese soup consisting of noodles, various vegetables, and meat in a flavorful broth. The dish gained popularity in restaurants after World War II. However, it was not perfected until 1958 when Momofuku Ando, founder of Nissin Foods and hero of college students and stoners the world over, invented the inexpensive instant version common today. In less time than it takes to pack a bowl and smoke it, one can prepare a delicious snack with enough sodium to kill a small horse that should cool off just in time to stave off the beginning phase of the munchies.

See also **Easy Mac**

Rasta Pasta, a form of pasta which can take on a variety of shapes, sizes, and flavor combinations, but always contains a particular type of herb that grants the eater increased powers of perception and understanding. The general method of delivery for the pot is to sauté it in oil or butter before adding additional spices to create the base for a sauce that is then poured over boiled noodles. The

© istockphoto / Elenathewise

layers of flavor found in most pasta dishes often mask the marijuana taste, so it can be difficult to detect the presence of weed in the dish. Just be patient, it's there.

Rice Krispies Treats, a popular stoner treat that is created simply by combining melted butter, melted marshmallows, and unmelted Rice Krispies cereal in a baking dish and allowing the concoction to cool. If one were so inclined, one could replace the boring unsalted butter with far less boring pot butter to create "Special Rice Krispies Treats." If doing so, it is very important that one makes the pot version before one gets high, not after. Getting high before could result in a scenario in which one comes down with the munchies just as the special treats are ready and overindulges. Eating one pot-laced dessert is fun. Eating ten is dangerous.

See also **pot butter**

Salt, a table condiment consisting of sodium and chlorine (sodium chloride) which adds flavor and texture to almost any food item and is one of the primary food groups for all stoners. Salt comes in a variety of strengths and flavors, such as table salt, sea salt, smoked sea salt, and kosher salt, among others. It is not only delicious but also essential in melting snow. It is also a compound which is required for the functioning of animal life, as it is a main bodily electrolyte, and it also helps in food preservation. In short, salt is a miracle. Too much salt intake may lead to high blood pressure and other health risks, though, but this is of no consequence to the recently inebriated. Stoners are known to pound through an entire bag of Frito-Lay potato chips and then reach for the Pringles tube before just emptying the salt shaker directly into their mouths and, finally, setting up an IV directly to their veins.

See also **Pringles**

Sandwiches, the chameleon of the munchie world, capable of taking on any number of shapes and ingredient combinations. One starts with a blank slate of two pieces of bread and builds the sandwich by shoving things like lettuce, tomato, ham, turkey, bologna, pickles, and bacon between the slices. This can be a simple process or a complex one, depending on the number of ingredients as well as the amount of cannabis consumed by the person making it.

© istockphoto / LauriPatterson

Sliced Bread, an essential ingredient in several stoner delicacies, including sandwiches and toast cream. It has been deemed to be such an amazing wonder of modern technology that it serves as a benchmark for all human accomplishments. That's right, in an era when one can call a friend 3,000 miles away while simultaneously streaming a video of two women doing unspeakable things with a single cup, people still look to sliced bread as the pinnacle of human achievement. Truth be told, the apple pipe is far more impressive.

Slurpee, a type of frozen beverage served at 7-Eleven convenience stores around the world. The ingenious concoction simply takes already successful drink flavors like Coca-Cola and cherry and converts them into a slushie. The drink is especially popular among stoners for several reasons: 1) It is cold, in contrast to hot marijuana smoke. 2) It is wet and alleviates cotton mouth. 3) It is available twenty-four hours a day. 4) When the cashier isn't looking, one can stick one's head under the nozzle and "wheeze the juice."

Smoothies, a beverage made by blending together fruit, yogurt, milk, and THC. The lecithin in the milk absorbs the THC, creating a sweet, healthy snack from which one can get high.

Sugar, nickname given to a lovely person and a primary edible table condiment that adds sweetness and flavor to most any food. Sugar comes in many forms, but the most widely used is the high fructose corn syrup that appears in soda, cookies, and so many other American food products. There is some debate about the health effects of high fructose corn syrup, with some calling it the primary force behind the

American obesity epidemic. Stoners call it the most flavorful joyride their tongue has ever experienced. Sugar is such a flavor enhancer that the only thing stopping stoners from eating an entire box of Frosted Flakes is the size of their stomachs and the terrible knowledge in the back of their heads that sugar may lead them to lose all their teeth, and thus never be able to eat Frosted Flakes again.

See also cereal

Taco Bell, a California-based purveyor of exotic foods like tacos, burritos, quesadillas, and other Mexican fare. Thanks to its speedy service and dirt-cheap prices, it has been a popular postsmoking destination since the 1960s. Skeptics question how the chain is able to provide edible food for as low as seventy-nine cents per item, and the answer is simple: It's better if one doesn't know. One should just enjoy the chalupa and try not to think about it.

See also KFC/Pizza Hut/Taco Bell

Toast Cream, a culinary experience best enjoyed under the influence of weed. One part toasted wheat bread, one part ice cream spread over aforementioned toasted bread, it yields a healthy snack that Martha Stewart is said to prepare for her guests following marathon sessions at her mansion. Invented in 1923 in Troy, New York, by the son of a vacuum salesman, toast cream has been applauded by stoners and gourmands the world over. Its simple ingredients and ease of assembly are perfectly suited to the childlike state one enters immediately after two large bong hits.

Twinkie, a popular baked good created by James Dewar in the 1930s, and currently distributed by the Hostess company. The snack consists of a spongy yellow cake that is filled with sweet vanilla cream. A popular urban legend states that, in the event of a nuclear war, the only remaining things on Earth would be roaches and Twinkies. Upon hearing said rumor, many stoners have trouble subsequently understanding why exactly nuclear war is such a bad thing.

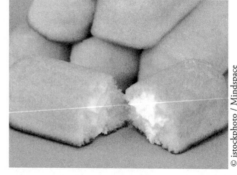

© istockphoto / Mindspace

Value Menu, a list of inexpensive items ranging from hamburgers to French fries to chicken nuggets, usually priced around $1, that can be found at various fast-food restaurants throughout the United States. Wendy's claims to have invented the concept in 1989 when it released the Super Value Menu, with Burger King and McDonald's refusing to officially enter the game until 1998 and 2002, respectively. Items from the value menu are an essential part of the stoner's diet due to their widespread availability and because their low cost allows the stoner to put money toward more important things. Like buying more pot.

Waffles, a breakfast food consisting of batter cooked to a golden crisp that is served at every waffle house in America. Waffles are best when combined with syrup. However, waffles are known to absorb the syrup when placed directly together. That's why experienced stoners who eat waffles know to put the syrup on the side and dip the waffle, maximizing the syrup's flavor. Waffles are also frequently combined with fruit, either by direct infusion (blueberry waffles, for example) or by cutting up the fruit and garnishing the waffles. The combination is perfect, as not only does it taste great but it also gives stoners the false sense that they're eating fruit and therefore a healthy meal. Thirty pounds later, they'll learn their lesson.

Wheezing the Juice, the practice of conspicuously sticking one's head underneath a Slurpee machine to pilfer large quantities of the frozen beverage. It was popularized by Pauly Shore in the cult classic *Encino Man* as he attempted to train a caveman in the stoner arts. This maneuver can be attempted only when high, as the reality of sucking artificially flavored slush from a hose will deter any self-respecting sober person.

See also **Slurpee**

White Castle, a restaurant founded in 1921 specializing in small hamburgers called sliders. Possibly aware that its tiny hamburgers make for ideal postsmoking munchies, the company often sells them in packages of thirty called "Crave Cases," practically daring smokers to test the limits of their stomach linings and eat an entire case in a single sitting. There is some debate over whether the name "slider" refers to how easily the tiny burgers slide into the stomach or how rapidly they slide out of it.

© istockphoto / HannamariaH